CLARE WHALLEY
META4 BUSINESS COACHING

COACHING BUSINESS OWNERS TO CREATE A BUSINESS YOU LOVE;
HELPING YOU WORK WITH YOUR IDEAL CLIENTS
AND EARN THE MONEY YOU WANT

DO. IT. NOW!

Copyright © 2020 by Clare Whalley
All rights reserved. This book or any portion thereof
may not be reproduced or used in any manner whatsoever
without the express written permission of the author
except for the use of brief quotations in a book review.

Website: www.meta4coaching.co.uk
Twitter: www.twitter.com/Meta4ltd
Facebook: www.facebook.com/meta4coaching
LinkedIn: www.uk.linkedin.com/in/clarewhalley

Welcome! 4
About Clare 5
Reviews for 'Do. It. Now!' 6
Who Loves You? 8
NLP Representational System Preference Quiz 9
Rep System Test Results 11
Neuro Linguistic Programming - Representational Styles 12
Your Values 13
Your Top 10 Values 14
Be Your Own Business Coach 15
Being Your Own Coach 17

Develop a Clear Action Plan 19
5 Rules to Follow When Setting Business Goals 20
Top 10 Tips for *Achieving* Your Goals 22
My Goal (an example) 23
Examples of 'Vision Boards' 24

Stand out from the crowd 26
Your Why 27
Creating a Business Mission Statement 28
Magic Marketing! 29
Defining Your Ideal Customer/Client 31
Your ideal client 33

Perfect Product & Service Offering 35
A Case Study - Developing a Product and Service Offering 36
Packaging up your services so customers can buy more easily from you 38
Calculating Your Worth 39
Examples of Business Packages 40

Gain Customers in the Short - Term (3-6 months) 43
Light Bulb Marketing Methods 44
More Marketing Ideas 45
How to write blog posts that get your business results 47
Setting 3-Month Goals 48

Gain Customers *Consistently* 49
10 Actions to Achieve More of the same juiciness... 50
Getting clear on your 12-Month Goals – Start with a plan of action 51
Keeping in Touch (with your customers) 52
Planning an E-Newsletter 53
My Story- Your 'Why' 55
I leaped into the Unknown 56
7 Steps to a Successful Sale 57

Share your Expertise 59
Delegating and Prioritising 60

Favourite Subjects Matrix 64

Generate Referrals 65
Client Feedback Form 66
Creating Referrals of a Lifetime 68
Examples of Warm Letters, Introductory Letters & Cards 70
Case Studies 73

Develop a Positive Mindset 75
Accomplishment List (My TaDa's) 76
Money Mindset and Beliefs 77
Urgent & Important Matrix 78
Daily Accountability Sheet 79
Dump it. Delegate it. Deal with it! 80

Develop Confidence & Self Belief 81
Accomplishments this year 82
Positive Self Image 83
Self Image O-Meter 84
Boost Your Confidence 85

Share Clear Messages 86
Developing a 60 Second Business Presentation 87
Top 10 Tips for Presenting 88
Top 10 Tips for Being a Great Networker 89
Case Study - 'Develop a scalable business; more focused implementation' 90

Selling Made Easy 91
Top 10 Tips to a Sustainable & Successful Business 92
Kick Start Business Pre-Qualifying Questions 93
Top 10 Mistakes to Avoid in your Job when Planning your Start-up 94
Start-Up Business Checklist 95
Beginner's Guide to Starting a Business in 3 Hours Per Week 96
The 5 Most Important Investments to Make in your Start-Up Business 97
Fun Stuff 98

Success Stories 99

Welcome!

Great work for purchasing this workbook. You are about to embark on a life and business-changing journey! I am pleased to be playing a part in that!

Thank you for purchasing **'Do. It. Now!'** - a refined set of strategies, that if you follow diligently will create a high level of focus, clarity and direction to develop your business into one you will love!

All the resources in this workbook also follow a 12-month coaching programme. The business owners who work with me directly use the resources in here throughout their coaching programme alongside their coaching sessions.

You can follow the resources and create great results without the coaching as long as you are a) fully committed to getting great business results b) keep yourself accountable to the tasks and are c) able to ask for help if and when you need it. Here's how:

You can follow me on my social media channels (see links below) and feel free to ask questions and seek advice as you use your 'Do. It. Now!' workbook.

> *"Alone we can do so little, together we can do so much."*
> *Helen Keller*

In the meantime, to get you off to the best start possible, go straight to page 12 and complete the Values Exercise. These will help lay the right foundations for you and your business' success.

I'm looking forward to helping you create more business success!

Clare

Join me online:
Website: www.meta4coaching.co.uk
Facebook: www.facebook.com/meta4coaching

Twitter: www.twitter.com/Meta4ltd
LinkedIn: www.uk.linkedin.com/in/clarewhalley

About Clare

I used to work for BT (is a well trotted out phrase for me!) I went more or less straight from University into their graduate scheme. At the time (1998) it was quite an accolade to get into their graduate scheme; tough application process, 3 tough interviews, psychometric tests, presentations, the lot; only a handful out of thousands got through. I was one of them. Even at that point I was utterly determined and equally committed to making sure I got in. The first 3 or 4 years were pretty amazing, lots of new friends, great pay raises, promotions, company car, free this and that...then the stress levels kicked in. You know, as you get more skilled and effective at your job, the more pressure and responsibility is piled on to you. I was managing BT Mobile's biggest account in Europe (worth over £60 million), a team of 25 people and then I was given another team to manage with another big account, and then another.

The Turning Point

Whilst a sadistic part of me enjoyed being the department's trouble-shooter and having the ability to turn poor performing teams and unhappy customers around, I knew this job and company was not for me. But what was?! In desperate times I went to see a Life Coach and suddenly, I got a huge amount of clarity. Resign. So, that's what I did. No job to go to, no money in the bank, married to a self-employed husband, but a clear idea that BT wasn't for me. But being a business owner was. Of course, at this point, I knew nothing about running my own business. Who does when you've never done it before?

Retrained

Immediately, I studied for 4 months and completed an NLP (Neuro-Linguistic Programming) course, which gave me the tools I needed to be a Life Coach and alongside my skills, strengths and experience managing customers, leading small and large teams and managing businesses within BT, I set up as a Life and Business Coach in July 2007. The next 3 years, starting with a recession, set me off on a huge learning curve. I struggled to make the money I wanted to make from my business, so found other sources of income relating to other skills I had; training and teaching. Determined to make my business successful, solely focused on coaching, I joined networking groups, read a myriad of personal and professional development books, attended business development courses, worked with a Business Coach myself and added to my business qualifications.

Now

Since 2007 I have worked with hundreds of business owners to help them create a more successful business - from chiropractic practices to social media specialists, from electrical businesses to coaches. Utilising all my learned skills (and failures) I have honed all best practices, strategies, tips and share them in here and through my coaching, so that my clients avoid all the unnecessary worry, stress, anxiety, sleepless nights and many failures; because they are unnecessary, if only you follow proven strategies, formulas and are always furnished with new ideas and ways to reach your ideal clients and are selling to them exactly what you want and they want!

So, here's to the next 12 months (that's how long it takes, as a minimum, to develop and create a successful, sustainable business) and beyond creating a business you will love!

Reviews for 'Do. It. Now!'

Since setting up in 2007 Clare has taken many businesses from standing still into the realms of growth and profitability.

This book has been born from her coaching programmes so you too can experience the power of an interactive programme.

This workbook has helped me to look closely at the current structure of my business and has highlighted where, why and how changes can be made to improve it. I now have systems in place that allow me to attract more of the clients I love to work with and do more of the work I enjoy doing. This gives me time to expand the services I offer to help and support more people. The book is structured in a way that makes it easy for me to follow and to add my thoughts and comments as a work through it. Its bite size chunks make working through it easy for me to put my full attention and focus onto one area at a time. The examples and templates provide great guidance to help me structure elements of my business.

Geoff Stokes

A well-structured book with great advice for business owners wanting to move their business forward. This book provides guidance and structure on how to get the most out of your business. Ultimately, it supports in creating a business that you love and how to ensure you are paid your worth. It covers topics such as goal setting, service offerings, marketing, sales, customer engagement, confidence building and much more. Its straightforward approach makes a lot of sense and the visual tables and forms throughout provide great templates so that you can replicate the exercises for your business. I would highly recommend this book for anyone looking to develop their business or anyone with a business idea they want to turn into a reality.

Alex Wheatherly, Virtual Business Support Services

A great step-by-step guide! I have loved using the Do it Now! Book that Clare has written. It has helped a complete business novice like me navigate my way through a complete maze of questions around beginning my business journey. There is a clear structure in the book that takes you through the basics of what you need to consider in starting out in business from a very practical perspective. The great thing is that the advice in the book works, it takes the pressure off and although there is a lot to learn, the ideas in the book will give you a solid base from which to grow your business.

Anita Oberoi, Headway Tuition Ltd

It works! A no nonsense workbook which is definitely helping me to gain positive results for my business. There is no padding or waffle - just practical steps which you can take TODAY to help you achieve your business potential. As a business owner who has never been engaged in marketing this has proved to be immensely helpful in making me take the first steps into using social media to help grow my client base. I'm writing this during the Covid pandemic, and I am finding the section on positive mindset really helpful at the moment!

Caroline Cook, Caroline Cook Financial Services Ltd

The 'Do. It. Now!' book has been an invaluable source of great resources to help develop my business ideas. It contains clear and concise information and examples to help apply Clare's knowledge & advice to your own business. The workbook gives you plenty of help to get your own ideas flowing and implement actions with easy to follow exercises; all you need to do is put the effort in.

Alex Dudley, D'Audio Music Group

A great collection of pointers and exercises to keep you and your business on track. Some of the exercises were completely new to me and others were very useful reminders. Clare's easy style keeps things simple and straightforward. I defy any business owner to pick this up and not find something useful.

Judith Hutchinson, Accessible Marketing

This workbook has helped me to look closely at the current structure of my business and has highlighted where, why and how changes can be made to improve it. I now have systems in place that allow me to attract more of the clients I love to work with and do more of the work I enjoy doing.

Sharon Taylor, Complete Harmony

I was given a copy of **'Do. It. Now!'** when I first started working with Clare. I took it home, started browsing through it and I was hooked! I found the book to be so comprehensive, clear, straightforward and user friendly, it covered everything, and I was excited!! I am in the early stages of starting my business, but I know with the help of this book I will be able to shape my business step by step, whilst ensuring I build it on a solid foundation. I trust this book and it's made me believe in the process, every time I pick it up, I'm motivated to do something which is quite something for someone who had procrastination down to an art form.

Kiran Thiara

A great book to keep your business on track…A great collection of pointers and exercises to keep you and your business on track. Some of the exercises were completely new to me and others were very useful reminders. Clare's easy style keeps things simple and straightforward. I defy any business owner to pick this up and not find something useful.

Amazon Customer

So Practical! So many business books are just telling you what to do and think, Clare's book is a way of getting your thoughts onto paper and making them reality. Goals into Reality! Thank you.

Katie Hale, Halestorm Business Development & Marketing

Who Loves You?

It obviously costs you less time (and money!) to (re)connect with people who already know about you and have previously enquired about your products and services. Take some time now to write down all the people who have expressed an interest in the services you offer, have used you before, or people who you feel would be interested in your services if only they knew about them. Once you have your list, have a think about what you can do next to 'Get in touch' and / or to re-engage with them. Book in for a coffee, connect on social media, give them a call etc.

Name	Contact Details	How do they know you? (Referral Source)	How will you get in touch? (1st touch)	How will you get in touch? (2nd touch)

'Who Loves You?' is adapted from Fabienne Fredrickson's 'Love 'em Up List'.

NLP Representational System Preference Quiz

Instructions:
For each of the following statements, please assign a number to every phrase. Use the following system to indicate your preferences:

1. Least descriptive of you
2. Next best description
3. Next best description
4. Best description of you

This short quiz will help you work out how you prefer to communicate and learn new things. It will also help you to understand how others prefer to communicate too.

If you have trouble deciding between two phases, go with the first thought that comes to mind.

1. When vacationing at the beach, the first thing that makes me glad to be there is:
a _ The feel of the cool sand, the warm sun or the fresh breeze on my face
b _ The roar of the waves, the whistling wind or the sound of birds in the distance
c _ This is the type of vacation that makes sense or the cost is reasonable
d _ The scenery, the bright sun, and the blue water

2. When I feel overwhelmed, I find it helps if:
a _ I can see the big picture
b _ I can talk or listen to another person
c _ I can get in touch with what is happening
d _ I make sense of things in my head

3. When given an assignment at work, it is easier to carry out if:
a _ I can picture what is required
b _ I have a feeling for what is required
c _ I have an understanding of what is required
d _ Someone talks to me about what is required

4. I find it easier to follow a presentation if:
a _ I feel in touch with the presenter and the material is within my grasp.
b _ There is a visual display so that I can visualize the concepts
c _ The presentation is based on facts and figures and is logically presented
d _ The presenter speaks clearly with varying tonality or uses sound to emphasize message

5. When buying a car, I make my decision on:
a _ The purchase price, gas mileage, safety features, etc.
b _ How comfortable the seats are or the feeling I get when I test drive it
c _ The colour, styling or how I would look in it
d _ The sound of the engine or stereo system or how quiet it rides

6. I communicate my thoughts through:
a _ My tone of my voice
b _ My words
c _ My appearance
d _ My feelings

7. When I am anxious, the first thing that happens is:
a _ Things begin to sound different
b _ Things begin to feel different
c _ Things begin to look different
d _ Things begin to not make sense

8. During a discussion, I am most influenced by:
a _ The other person's logic
b _ The other person's tone of voice
c _ The energy I feel from the other person
d _ Seeing the other person's body language or being able to picture the other person's viewpoint

9. I assess how well I am doing at work based on:
a _ My understanding of what needs to be done
b _ How I see myself making progress
c _ The tone of voice used by my colleagues and superiors
d _ How satisfied I feel

10. One of my strengths is my ability to:
a _ See what needs to be done
b _ Make sense of new facts and data
c _ Hear what sounds right
d _ Get in touch with my feelings

11. It is easiest for me to:
a _ Select the volume, base and treble for easy listening on a stereo system
b _ Select the an intellectually relevant point in a conversation
c _ Select comfortable furniture
d _ Select rich, attractive colour combinations

12. If you agree with someone, are you more likely to say:
a _ That feels right
b _ That looks right.
c _ That sounds right.
d _ That makes sense.

Rep System Test Results

For each question on the previous pages note your answers in the box with the appropriate letter. In other words, if you wrote down 4 where the D is on question 1 (Visual). Repeat for every answer.

Question Number	Visual	Auditory	Kinaesthetic	Auditory Digital (LOGICAL)
1	d 4	b	a	c
2	a	b	c	d
3	a	d	b	c
4	b	d	a	c
5	c	d	b	a
6	c	a	d	b
7	c	a	b	d
8	d	b	c	a
9	b	c	d	a
10	a	c	d	b
11	d	a	c	b
12	b	c	a	d
Total	V=	A=	K=	Ad=

The comparison of the total scores in each column will give the relative preference for each of the 4 major representational systems.

Neuro Linguistic Programming - Representational Styles

In NLP terms; Visual, Auditory, Kinaesthetic and Auditory Digital words are called predicates. The predicates or words that a person uses will provide you with an indication of the person's preferred representational system – how they prefer to communicate or learn. You will easily recognise yourself in these styles and words.

Visual - learn by memorising pictures, interested in how things look and they bored with long verbal explanations.

Auditory – learn by listening, tone of voice is important. Words used are important

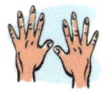

Kinaesthetic – respond by physical rewards. Memorise by doing; walking through things. Interested in things that feel right, that give a gut feeling.

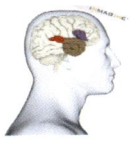

Auditory Digital – Need to make sense of things, needs to be logical. Often talk to themselves, think things through in their heads. Need to talk things through with other people.

Which communication style do you prefer?

Important to understand the styles so you can ensure you focus on all 4 styles in your marketing and communication etc.

Visual	Auditory	Auditory Digital	Kinaesthetic
see	hear	sense	grasp
look	tell	experience	feel
bright	sound	understand	hard
clear	resonate	change	unfeeling
picture	listen	perceive	concrete
foggy	silence	question	scrape
view	deaf	insensitive	solid
clear	squeak	distinct	touch
focused	hush	conceive	get hold of
dawn	roar	know	catch argument
reveal	melody	think	pull some strings
illuminate	make music	learn	sharp on
imagine	harmonize	process	tap into
hazy	tune in/out	decide	heated as a tack
an eyeful	rings a bell	motivate	smooth operator
short sighted	quiet as a mouse	consider	make contact
sight for sore eyes	voiced an opinion	describe in detail	throw out
take a peek	clear as a bell	figure it out	firm foundation
tunnel vision	give me your ear	make sense of	get a handle on
bird's eye view	loud and clear	pay attention to	get in touch with
naked eye	purrs like a kitten	word for word	hand in hand
paint a picture	on another note	without a doubt	hang in there

12

Your Values

"It's not hard to make decisions when you know what your values are."
— **Roy Disney**

Research shows those who know their values and have them aligned across their personal and professional life are happier, more fulfilled and therefore more successful in what they do.

Select the **Top 10-12 values** you feel mostly reflect how you currently live your personal and professional life. What are the 10 – 12 most important values to you? Once you have these you can place them in order of importance.

An insightful exercise to complete next is to 'traffic light' your selected values.

For example:

- You may feel the value you have selected is important to you, but you have little to none of it reflected in your personal and professional life. This value goes in to **RED**.
- You may feel the value you have selected is important to you, and whilst you have a bit of that value reflected in your personal and professional life, you know you could have more of it. This goes into **AMBER**.
- You may believe the value you have selected is important to you AND it is currently throughout all of what you do, personally and professional. Congratulations, this part of your life is working well. This value goes into **GREEN**.

Accomplishment	Discovery	Romance	Rule of Law
Accountability	Ease of Use	Loyalty	Safety
Accuracy	Efficiency	Maximum utilisation (of time, resources)	Satisfying others
Achievement	Equality		Security
Adventure	Excellence	Meaning	Self-giving
All for one & one for all	Fairness	Merit	Self-reliance
Beauty	Faith	Money	Service
Calm	Family	Openness	Simplicity
Challenge	Financial Freedom	Orderliness	Skill
Change	Flair	Peace, Non-violence	Speed
Cleanliness,	Freedom	Perfection	Spirit in life
Collaboration	Friendship	Personal Growth	Stability
Commitment	Fun	Pleasure	Standardisation
Communication	Global view	Positive attitude	Status
Community	Good will	Power	Strength
Competence	Goodness	Practicality	Succeed; a will to-
Competition	Gratitude	Preservation	Success
Concern for others	Hard work	Privacy	Systemisation
Content over form	Harmony	Problem Solving	Teamwork
Continuous improvement	Honesty	Progress	Timeliness
Cooperation	Honour	Prosperity	Tolerance
Coordination	Independence	Punctuality	Tradition
Country, love of	Inner peace	Quality of work	Tranquillity
Creativity	Innovation	Quietude	Trust
Customer satisfaction	Integrity	Regularity	Truth
Decisiveness	Justice	Resourcefulness	Unity
Delight of being, joy	Knowledge	Respect for others	Variety
Democracy	Leadership	Responsiveness	Wisdom
Discipline	Love	Results-oriented	Wealth

Your Top 10 Values

1.   6.
2.   7.
3.   8.
4.   9.
5.   10.

Now that you have your top 10 values in order and you are clear on what you want and *need* more of in your personal and professional life, i.e. those values that are marked in red and orange. The values in red and orange are giving you clarity - showing you where your gaps are.

This means you can now start planning for what you need to do in order to get more alignment with your values; getting you closer to them all being marked green…more happiness, fulfilment and personal and professional success.

Be Your Own Business Coach
Stop working so hard and start achieving more!

Having the business you desire can be made easier – as long as you have just that: **DESIRE**; to achieve it, you follow your instincts and are open to opportunities; however they present themselves. You are prepared to take action and have accountability for your goals. Here I'm addressing the 5 commonly posed problems from the business owners I work with. Ready...?

These are the solid foundations to any business. Get clarity on each of these and you have the right foundations in place to build upon for a successful business:

1. How do I set goals?
Firstly, understand what is it that you want to achieve. Setting goals is a key part to moving forward with any major change. Understand *what* it is you want. And *how* you will get there – what steps could you take to get you closer. Then start **taking action**! Start this process by waving a magic wand, imagine there are no obstacles, no limiting beliefs – you can have exactly what you want! This is your starting point to follow through with what really makes you tick / want to leap out of bed to get on with / your passion and driving force.

2. Finding Clients - Who are your ideal customers?
An obvious question often overlooked by business owners; **HOWEVER**, *so, so* important! Think about your ideal customer, that person you love/loved working with. Now, what do you know about them? How did they feel before they started working with you, how do they feel after working with you: what problems did you help them solve, where do they hangout, why are they choosing to work with you? **Write down everything you know about them.** This is the valuable copy and content you will use in your marketing to attract more of the people you can make a difference with and who need your services.

3. Closing prospects
Make it a foregone conclusion. The (potential) client has approached you, so there must be something that they're interested in buying from you, finding out more about. Again, think about your ideal client – how did they initially buy from you, what process did they go through? If in doubt go back and ask them. Go on! Be brave and then you can replicate the process. Also see my '7 Steps to a Successful Sale' and 'Marketing to Close' Process for what your decision maker goes through in order to say YES.

4. How do I demonstrate my credibility?
Be the expert. Believe in yourself! If you don't, how will your customer? Fortunately, confidence is a learned skill. Give yourself a boost; write down everything you've achieved. Ask your customers for testimonials about your products and services and believe them! Add lots of value to your service offering and then be confident to step outside of your comfort zone and share the greatness your service helps others achieve.

5. How can I create a passive income?
Every business owner's dream, right? Earning while not 'working'. What can you offer to your customers that can be packaged up and sold wherever and whenever in the world? Think creatively. This idea may not jump & hit you in the face: it can take a while. So, write the question down, put it out there and keep coming back to it. How can I create a passive income? Jot down all the ideas you have, however small, large, silly or otherwise. Then select the top one that fits most with who you want to work with, what you want to be sharing and what's the 1st small step to creating that product / service?

What is the 1st action you will take from this exercise?

What is the 2nd action you will take from this exercise?

Being Your Own Coach

Learning how to be more *insert desired skill* or have more *insert desired attribute* doesn't have to be difficult. It just must be **desired**, **acted on**, **be practiced** and **focused upon**. Here are my 5 top tips for actions you can take to understand what it's like to work with a coach, to be your own coach and how to start moving forward. Coaching is about taking action and having accountability for your goals. Writing your goals down will make them 42% more likely to happen.

Top 5 Tips for Being your Own Coach

1. **Understand your blockage/s** – what is currently getting in the way of you moving forward? 1) Are you making excuses, 2) are your values, rules for life, aligned with your personal and professional life, 3) do you have all the resources, skills you need for your change, 4) is something from your past stopping you from moving forward? Once you understand the blockage – it becomes easier to understand how to remove it.

2. **Purchase a journal or notebook** – start to make notes about your current thoughts. Whatever they are, don't question them, just write them down. This gives you clarity, a different perspective, helps you to find your own solutions to problems. If you don't journal already, you'll be amazed at how it helps you find answers and solace.

3. **Use affirmations** – Your subconscious mind is 30,000 times more powerful than your conscious mind. Think about what you're aiming to achieve and create a strong, powerful sentence or statement to reflect that; e.g. 'I am losing weight and becoming fitter and healthier every day.' You don't have to believe your affirmation at first, in fact it's highly likely that you won't! Write the affirmation down, keep it close to you and keep repeating, especially when negative thoughts start to creep in.

4. **Use the Law of Attraction** – ever heard the phrase you reap what you sow? The law of attraction is the thinking: everything that happens to you as a result of your own thoughts and actions. There are some great apps that help you practice this train of thought. Check out 'Esther Hicks' as your starting point. Think about and visualise what it is you want to achieve. Really practice what this looks like, feels like, sounds like and focus on this thought throughout your day, week, month etc.

5. **Set Goals** – setting goals is a key part to moving forward with change. First understand *what* it is you want. The *how* will start to become clearer for you – note down a few ideas for the how's and then start **taking action…**

Use this space to note your **blockages** – what obstacles are currently getting in the way of you moving forward?

What is the 1st action you will take to start removing your blockages?

Develop a Clear Action Plan

Any starting point to major change regarding personal or professional development must start with planning. What do you want to achieve, change or develop? This section will help you to get the plans out of your head, on to paper and into action.

5 Rules to Follow When Setting Business Goals

What gets in the way of you achieving your business goals? Mostly it' because business owners rarely have them. There are easy ways to set goals - brainstorming what you want to achieve is the best way to start. And the best way to combat the obstacles that will inevitably come up is to keep to these 5 golden rules:

Rule No. 1 - Believe in yourself and your goals
Especially if you're setting bold goals, or you've set them before and haven't achieved them. You must relinquish all thoughts of the obstacles and barriers to your achievement and BELIEVE you can achieve. **Combat the Obstacle** = Create an affirmation/positive statement in the here and now, which affirms your goal, e.g. '**I am** running a successful business earning….' '**I am** attracting more of the clients I love to work with…' **I am…**'

Rule No. 2 - Only be reliant upon yourself when setting your goals.
Of course, others can be included WHEN you've achieved and celebrating the fruits of your achievements, but only include yourself in the actions to be taken. **Combat the Obstacle** = get the buy in from person/s you wish to involve in the end result. They may wish to create their own actions to help achieve the goal too. Finding out 'why' they want to achieve it too will add gravitas to your goals.

Rule No. 3 - Keep your business goals in line with your personal goals.
It's no good having business goals that are going to be detrimental to the enjoyment of your personal life. No one was ever happy being a lonely millionaire! **Combat the Obstacle** = write down a list of your top 10 personal and professional values (rules for which you run your life – see 'Your Values') and always keep these in mind when setting your goals.

Rule No. 4 - Make your goals bold and realistic.
If you're setting monetary goals, establish a figure (see 'How Much Should I be Charging for My Business Services') and work backwards how do the numbers add up: how many clients, customers, products, services do you need to sell on a daily, weekly and monthly basis? **Combat the Obstacle** = Live those figures; have them as part of your daily thoughts, affirmations, find other innovative ways to make them happen - price increase, new products and services, added value etc.

Rule No. 5 - Take Action.
Some personal development books may point towards you just *thinking* about what you want to achieve and then you magically achieving them. Yes, the law of attraction works, but you must act on your goals to *really* make the magic happen. **Combat the obstacle** = take small steps; take them steps every day to break down the bigger goals to make them happen!

Jot down your ideas and obstacles here and start to overcome them...

Top 10 Tips for *Achieving* Your Goals

1. **Set Goals!!** Only 5% of our population set goals, so if you're about to embark on this, good for you – you're in a fabulous minority! We've already mentioned you are 42% more likely to achieve goals that are written down. Use your time to think about what you want to achieve in the next 12 months. Use one (or large) paper for 'why you want to achieve, 'what' you want to achieve. Then 'how'.

2. **Make your goals visual and k**eep your goals close by to you**.** Move them around from time to time, so you are always 'seeing' your goals. Keep re-reading and addressing the 'how's'.

3. **Create a vision board (see point above)** for your goals to make them real and tangible. Gather pictures, images that reflect your goals. Place somewhere prominent.

4. **Share your goals with a trusted friend, partner or colleague.** By sharing your goals, it gives you more accountability towards achieving them.

5. **Be Bold.** Create goals that really excite you. They should fill you with inspiration, excitement, and passion and (at the same time) be a little bit scary for you. Goals are achieved outside of our comfort zone.

6. **Put small manageable steps, with deadlines, in place for your goals.** These will ensure you keep on track, give you momentum and provide you with the feeling of moving forward; giving you that much needed motivation and accountability!

7. **Make sure your goals are across all areas of your personal and professional life.** Which helps you map out your 'why'. Why do you want to achieve them? You're much more likely to go for, and achieve, if your goals are across all areas of your life.

8. **Get the experts in.** We all need help with what we're aiming to achieve something we have never done before. From a coach, to a trainer, to mentors, to a book. Think about your goals carefully and never be afraid to ask for help - it's right out there waiting for you once you ask.

9. **Use an array of tools for mapping out your goals**: handwritten, vision boards, mind maps - both hand and computer led. Find out what works for you.

10. **Maintain a positive mindset.** Use the Law of Attraction to help you – get clarity and focus and be intentional. Use your imagination, gratitude and the feeling of 'already having' to help get you closer to achieving your goals. The power of self-belief and confidence in achievement will help you to make it happen!

Jot down your ideas here...

My Goal (an example)

Here's an example of a written goal a past client of mine wrote out and read and re-read and took small action steps towards before they achieved it. Hope it inspires…

It's July 1st 2005 and I am sitting in my 5 bedroom, detached, neo-Georgian house near Guildford. The lounge is 45 feet long and 25 feet wide and the floors throughout the house are oak. The room is decorated in pastel shades of green, blending in perfectly with the French curtains and the Italian furniture.

There is a spacious feel about the whole house as each room is large allowing a sense of freedom. Each room is decorated to my taste and I am delighted with the overall feel of the house.

I can see the garden through the window, the beautifully manicured lawns bordered by borders filled with summer blossoms. As I smell the scents of the garden floating in through the French windows I reflect back at the time 3 years ago when I wrote this goal and recall the first step of the journey to this house when I set up my own practice.

As I sit here now I have a real sense of achievement, a feeling of well-being and excitement of finally achieving some of my potential.

The house is mortgaged to 50% of its value on the day I purchased it.

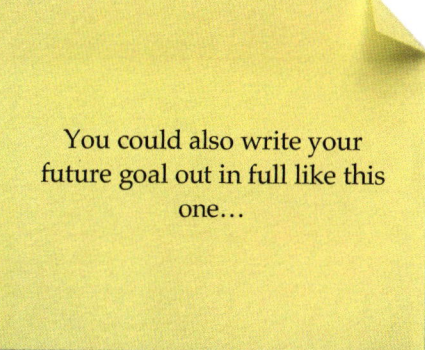

You could also write your future goal out in full like this one…

Examples of 'Vision Boards'

Stand out from the crowd

Time to get crystal clear on your ideal customer, to underpin all your marketing activity and materials. How to get your ideal customers chomping at the bit to work with you, as you are just the person to help them get the results they are looking for.

Your Why

This is an important exercise to get you clarity around why you do the business you do. People buy emotionally, so to connect to your why and share it will help others easily understand and connect with you.

So, ask yourself this - if you could leave this world in a better place than before, what would it look like for you? This is your why…

My Why: _____

Here's My *Why*…
(Why) I have invested my heart and soul and thousands of pounds into learning all it takes to run a successful small business so other business owners don't have to. My urgent challenge is to guide more business owners through the complex to the simplicities of building a business that gives financial freedom, motivation, balance and fulfilment.

Why:

Here's My *How* I do what I do…
(How) By delivering structured coaching programmes that have all the answers to running a successful business

How:

Here's my *What* do I do…
(What) Coaching business owners to run a business in a way they've always dreamed of.

What:

Creating a Business Mission Statement

Your **company's mission statement** is your opportunity to define your **company's** goals, ethics, culture, and norms for decision-making in a few words or a succinct sentence.

Mission statements allow businesses to define and establish their brand, telling their audience exactly what the company does, and how, in as concise and specific a way as possible.

They help potential clients relate to you and your company more easily.

Company Mission Statement Examples:

Zest Chiropractic:
A fun and energetic team, passionate about health and wellness. We want you to live a happy, healthy, pain-free life and will support you all the way. With the right nutrition, exercise, mindset and an optimally functioning spine and nervous system you really do have the power to take control of your wellbeing naturally.

Amazon:
It's our goal to be Earth's most customer-centric company, where customers can find and discover anything they might want to buy online.

Chanel:
To be the ultimate house of luxury, defining style and creating desire, now and forever.

Create your own mission statement

> Start by jotting down the 3 key values reflect you both personally and professionally. Jot down words / statements that reflect you and see how that develops:

Magic Marketing!

Start by focusing on what keeps your ideal client awake at night. This exercise means going to a depressing place first (it has to – you're solving problems!) but it'll soon turn around into how you can help.

What are your client's biggest problems? Focus on that problem, it usually has branches, i.e. problems because of that one problem.

_____

_____

_____

Connect with your audience
This is a great tool for understanding your main challenges and ensuring your marketing activities 'speak' to them directly.

What are the 3 consequences for your client if this problem does not get solved?

1. _____
2. _____
3. _____

What are your client's next biggest problems? Focus on that problem; it usually has branches, i.e. problems because of that one problem.

_____

_____

_____

What are the 3 consequences for your client if this problem does not get solved?

1. _____
2. _____
3. _____

What are your client's next biggest problems? Focus on that problem; it usually has branches, i.e. problems because of that one problem.

_____

_____

_____

What are the 3 consequences for your client if this problem does not get solved?

1. _____
2. _____
3. _____

Now, turn these problems/negatives into positives and solutions. How can you use these problems to demonstrate solutions and the positive (should they choose to address them). You can do this through: blogs, vlogs, articles to engage your clients and let them know you can *solve* their challenges and take away their pain?

e.g. **Problem**: Potential client has lost all control in their business
    Problem: is now too busy to focus on developing their business
    Problem: is stressed and unable to concentrate on the important bits they love
    Consequence: Potential client is missing important customer interaction
    Consequence: Is not spending any time to grow or develop himself/herself or the business
    Consequence: Is being kept awake at night and is feeling tired and irritable most of the time
    Blog/Vlog/Article Idea/s: 5 Steps to gain the control back in your business

Now, your turn:

Defining Your Ideal Customer/Client

This exercise will help underpin all your marketing, so it's important to get as clear as you possibly can with all the details of your 'Ideal Client.' Start by thinking about a client you have worked with in the past and if you could work with this person/s all day, every day, then your business would look and feel amazing! If you are starting out, think about the kind of client you would love to work with. This exercise is based on an exercise shared by Claire Mitchell's 'The Girls Mean Business'. Start by developing One – Two client profiles. Write down everything you know about them…

Who Are They? **Customer No.1** Attributes/Personality Traits, Geography, Specific Language use, Gender, Age bracket, Industry, Demographic etc.	Who Are They? **Customer No.2** Attributes/Personality Traits, Geography, Specific Language use, Gender, Age bracket, Industry, Demographic etc.
What problems do/could you solve for them?	What problems do/could you solve for them?

How do/could you make them feel?	How do/could you make them feel?
Where do they hang out?	**Where do they hang out?**

Actions:

Your ideal client

You need to know and understand YOUR ideal client inside out. This will show them you can solve their issues. We buy based on trust.

What problem do you solve for them?

Who are they? Geography, gender, age, industry, personality traits…?

How do you make them feel? What emotions will they rid and have as a result of working with you?

Where do they hang out? What publications, magazine, sites do they visit?

33

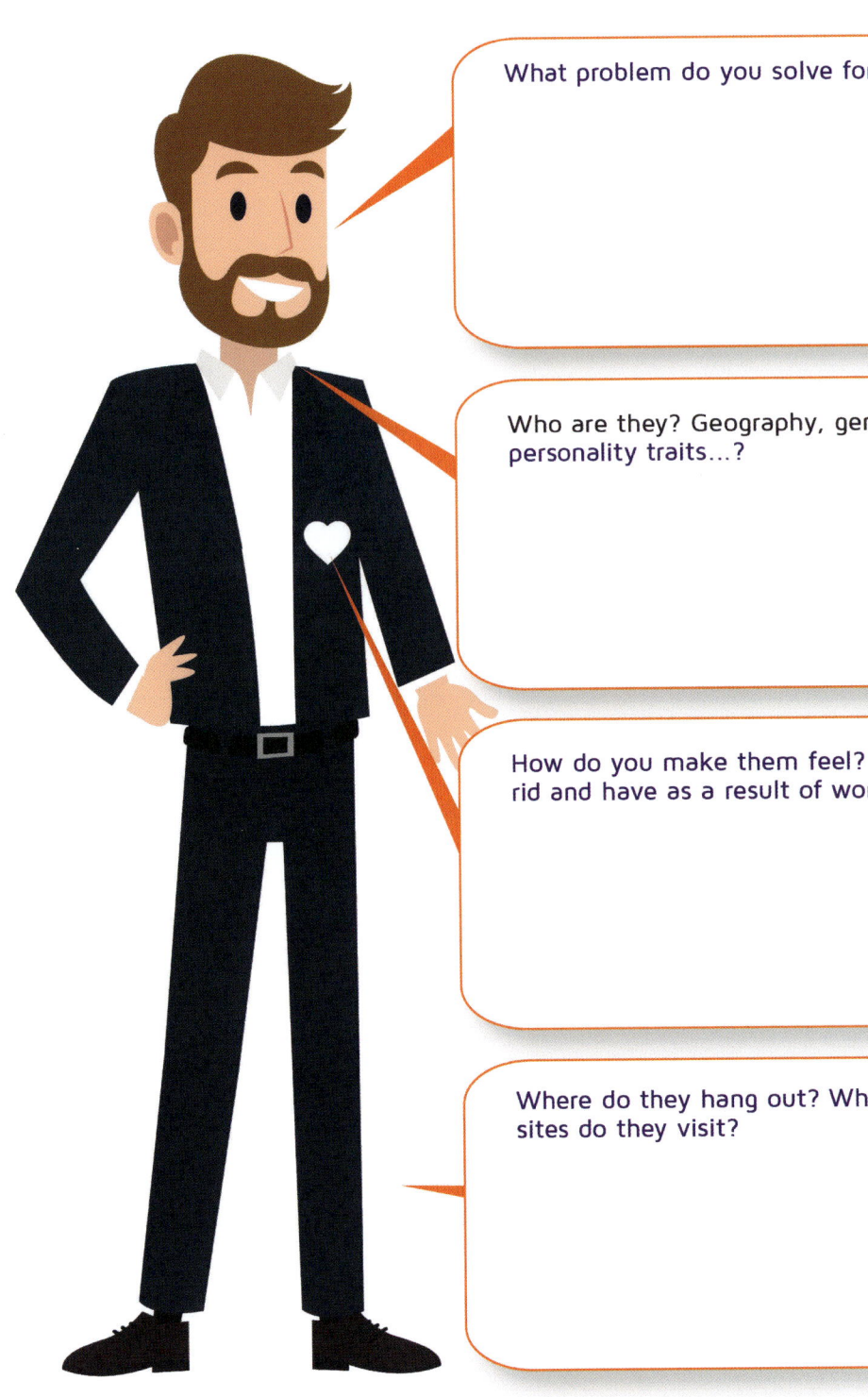

Perfect Product & Service Offering

Once you're clear on *who* you want to be working with, it's time to develop a compelling suite of (products and) services that deliver exactly what you want to offer and what your ideal customers want (and need) to buy from you. This will help you to create monthly income streams and higher end customer investments.

A Case Study - Developing a Product and Service Offering

Make it as easy as possible for customers to do business with you.

I often hear business owners who are getting enquiries, meeting with potential clients who are interested in what they do and appear to want to work with them, but for some reason the business owners is unable to close the sale and get the client to go ahead.

This is often down to the fact that the customer doesn't really know how to engage with you, what the service looks, sounds, feels like to them. How often will they be working with you, for how long, how much will the investment be and what results will they achieve working with you? All these questions need answers, so that the client has a crystal-clear understanding in their minds. This is especially important with a service led business, which often has intangible results. Developing a clear product and service suit will bridge this gap. Here's how packaging up her service offering worked for one of my client's business...

Sharon Taylor - Complete Harmony

Complete Harmony aims to provide a place where you can relax and unwind in the knowledge that you are in the safe and caring hands of an expert complementary therapist, providing treatments that will work alongside conventional medicine in a safe and complementary way.

What challenges were you experiencing in your business before you came to see me; before you packaged up what you offer?

I didn't have a clear enough idea of who my ideal clients were. I wasn't confident in explaining to clients how more than one treatment would benefit them as I didn't have a structure in place for retaining clients; therefore, I was only seeing clients for one off treatments.

What positive results are you experiencing in your business now you have packaged your services?

1. The packages have given me more self-confidence when I share what I can do for each client and when talking about my business at networking events.
2. I have a clear structure in terms of what I can offer on each package.
3. I'm able to offer clients structured programme to help them with their challenges
4. I am now working with more of the clients I love to work with.
5. Increased number of clients.
6. Previous clients returning to invest in themselves by buying packaged sessions.
7. A new client via a recommendation investing in themselves by purchasing a treatment package.
8. Packages being purchased as gifts instead of a one-off gift voucher.

In monetary terms what is the percentage increase in your average customer spend with you?

Now I'm asking clients would they like a package of 3, 6 or 9 treatments? Most who have booked a package are having a 3 treatment package which would equate to just an increase in nearly 300%.
80% of all my new clients on packages have rebooked, of those rebooked they have increased their spend with me and opted for longer term solutions to their challenges.

What positive difference have the packages made to your clients experience?

Clients are booking packages, as it is a more cost effective way to book rather than an off one treatment or one at a time. They have fed back they like to get their treatments booked in advance at a time that is good for them. Clients are feeling better after each visit as it's so relaxing and calming. They are reminded of the importance of incorporating relaxation and self-care into their daily, weekly, monthly life to help with de-stressing, re-energising and regaining balance.

What positive difference have the packages made to you and your business overall?

- ☐ *The packages give me a structure to work with and I can still tailor each package to the client. I now have the confidence to offer clients a programme of sessions with achievable outcomes.*
- ☐ *I'm working with more of the people I love working with as they are looking for a structured, targeted approach.*
- ☐ *I now don't have as many people asking discounts as they can see that the packages offer excellent value.*
- ☐ *I have to attract fewer new clients.*
- ☐ *I am now able to have a regular weekly treatment clinic in Tamworth.*
- ☐ *Client referrals have increased.*
- ☐ *A new client purchased monthly packages to be delivered over 9 week. The package was reviewed mid-way and at completion. After the 9 weeks the client was impressed with the progress and booked weekly treatments for the next 8 months.*

What are the *benefits* of packaging up your products and services?

Packaging up your services so customers can buy more easily from you

- Your customer wants to feel they are the ones in control of their buying and that they have choices and options available to them.
- You should find this exercise a challenge and it will be always a changing offering, as your experience levels change, qualifications are added, more knowledge is acquired etc.
- Once you have packages in place 'selling' and sharing your services will be much easier and clearer and as a result your customer will buy from you more readily - Remember a confused customer never buys.

1) Who is this package created for?
Put your ideal customer at the forefront at all times. The package must speak directly to the person it is ideally made for, think about the language you use so it speaks directly to them.

2) What results will your customers get?
What results does your ideal customers really want from you? How do they want to feel, what results do they want to receive? Ask them, do a survey and once you've found the answers to those questions you can map out what results your packages will deliver.

3) What services will be delivered?
This is your lovely business, so an all important question; what do *you* want to deliver to your customers and how do you want to deliver it in order to get them the best results?

4) What are the associated investments?
Be clear and confident with the associated investments. Give your customer options of how they may pay, i.e. monthly, upfront, spread etc. Think back to when you made an important purchase; were you able to spread the costs? How?

5) Develop 3 Choices
Offer three levels or three choices of *what* services your customer can buy from you and how they choose to receive the service. 1) A top, all singing, all dancing option, 2) a middle of the road and 3) an entry option that will also give the receiver great results.

See package examples to spark lots of ideas

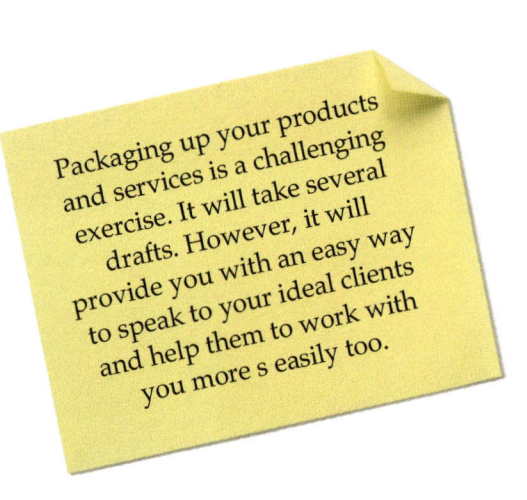

One of the most important triggers in attracting and gaining new clients for service led businesses...

Packaging up your products and services is a challenging exercise. It will take several drafts. However, it will provide you with an easy way to speak to your ideal clients and help them to work with you more s easily too.

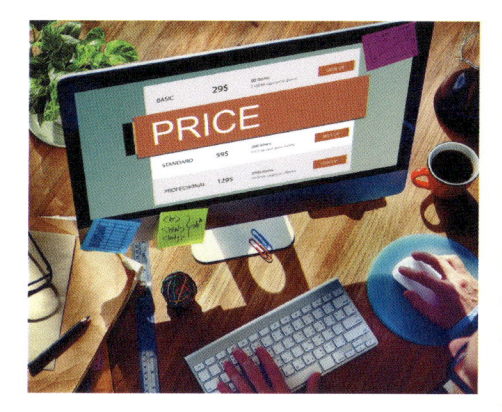

Calculating Your Worth

This often presents a challenge for business owners, especially for start-ups. Where do you get your prices from? How and where do you start?

Use this help sheet as your starting point.

Do's

★ Take into consideration courses, learning, experience you have in your field of expertise
★ Ignore what your competitors are offering. Yes, be aware, of their product and service offering, but differentiate yourself and **ADD VALUE**
★ Stretch yourself. Your pricing structure should feel bold and exciting
★ Package up your product and service offering. If you're a service led business, give your customers a choice on what they buy from you, in terms of cost and delivery methods
★ Fairly calculate your cost to serve: the time it takes for you to fully deliver your offering
★ Use a workable calculation - see below

Don'ts

☐ Underestimate the value or return a client working with you will get. Is it a life-time, life-changing return?
☐ Judge your potential customers buying power or decision making. They have a completely different set of beliefs and circumstances to you and are buying what you have to offer for their own reasons.

5 Step Daily Rate Calculator (thanks to Deb Golec of Papillion Coaching for allowing me to adapt and share)

Step 1: Desired annual income - be realistic, yet bold. Example: £50,000
Step 2: Calculate the number of days you are available to work (take into account holidays)
Example: 15 days per month x 12 = 180 days per year
Step 3: Daily Rate. Divide your desired annual income by the number of days available to work.
Example: £50,000 / 180 = £278.00
Step 4: Expenses/Cost to run your business per day. Include all costs. Calculate an annual figure and divide by number of days available to work.

Office Costs -
Personnel -
Marketing -
Training -
Pensions -
Car costs -
Total Costs - £4,000 / 180 = £22.00
Add this to your daily rate £22 + £278 = £300.00

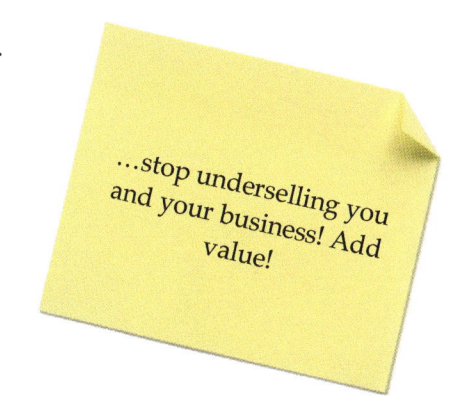

Step 5: Is your daily rate figure offering value for money to your customers? Is it realistic?

...stop underselling you and your business! Add value!

Space to start a plan:

Examples of Business Packages
Ark Media

ARK MEDIA PRODUCTIONS

Video production for small business

An affordable video production package for small business, our Indie Flick service covers everything you need to create an engaging, quality corporate video, without a Hollywood budget. It's simple to get started: our experts will discuss your brief and ways to present your video. Our film editing experts will then create a 60-second promotional video, ideal as a web video, promotional video or as part of your business presentations.

Box Office Hit: *Business films with impact*

The Box Office Hit package is perfect for creating promotional business films with impact. You get access to our seasoned scriptwriters, project directors, voiceover artists and web developers, as well as a longer video (up to two minutes) and a full day of filming. The Box Office Hit package makes corporate video production a simple, pain-free process, with professional film editing to create a promotional video which really hits home with your customers and colleagues.

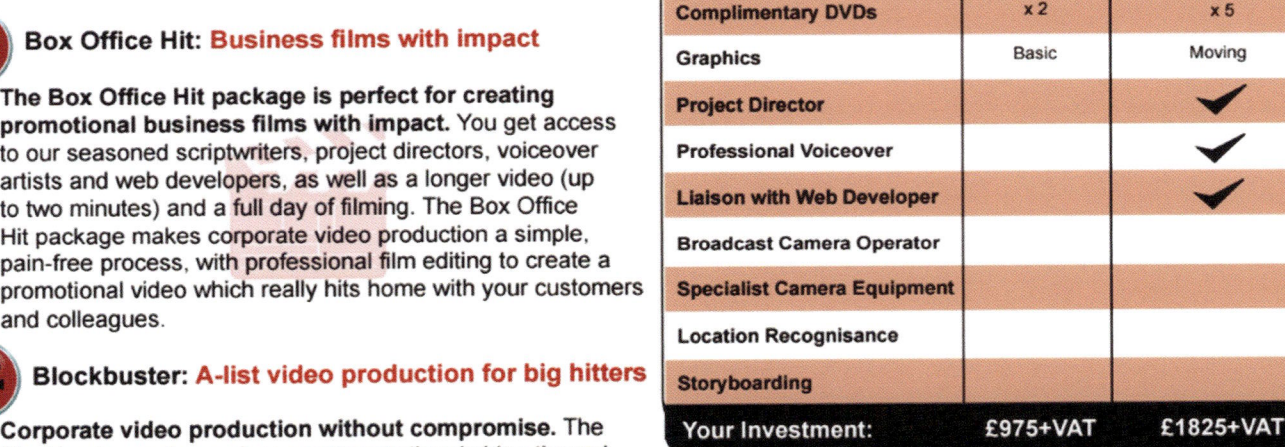

Blockbuster: *A-list video production for big hitters*

Corporate video production without compromise. The Blockbuster package gives your promotional video the red carpet treatment. Create a marquee movie with glitz and glamour, and make your video marketing a must-watch for customers, competitors and cinema connoisseurs! The Blockbuster package delivers the immersive, engaging experience of a Hollywood classic, with specialist equipment, free DVDs, storyboarding, and bespoke filming to meet all your requirements.

> Some working examples of successfully working business packages

	Indie Flick	Box Office Hit	Blockbuster
Project management	✓	✓	✓
Structuring of Film	✓	✓	✓
Script Writing		✓	✓
Filming	Half day	1 day	3 days
HD camera	✓	✓	✓
Film Length	60 secs	90-120 secs	3-5 Minutes
Complimentary DVDs	x 2	x 5	x 10
Graphics	Basic	Moving	Full Animated
Project Director			✓
Professional Voiceover		✓	✓
Liaison with Web Developer		✓	✓
Broadcast Camera Operator			✓
Specialist Camera Equipment			✓
Location Recognisance			✓
Storyboarding			✓
Your Investment:	£975+VAT	£1825+VAT	£3995+VAT

@ARKMEDIAPRODS   0845 519 3904   WWW.ARKMEDIA.CO.UK   info@ARKMEDIA.CO.UK   ARK MEDIA PRODUCTIONS

Zest Healthcare

ZEST HEALTHCARE PLANS

Health is your most valuable possession. It affects everything you do and everyone you know. Our care recommendations are based on our knowledge and experience of what works best for your individual case. The question is - how healthy do you want to be?

Superior – let's get you moving

Our superior care plan is ideal for new conditions and people whose general health is good. We will help get you moving again, get you off your pain relief medication and starting to return to doing the things you love.

Deluxe – beat chronic problems, feel stronger

If your symptoms are recurring or your underlying problem has been present for a few months then this is a great plan to get you feeling fantastic again. This comprehensive package is suitable people who want to achieve more and really start getting their life back. Our corrective exercises will stabilize your spine and nervous system and help prevent relapses in your condition.

Amazing – be the best you can be

If your symptoms have been off and on for years, and you're really committed to getting into great condition, then our amazing healthcare plan is for you. With our advanced rehab exercises, lifestyle and nutritional advice we can really help you feel fantastic and start living life to your full potential. Take control of your health and your future and be the best you can be!

	Superior	Deluxe	Amazing
Adjustment sessions	12	18	24
Time frame	8 weeks	12 weeks	14-16 weeks
Improved pain	✓	✓	✓
Better movement	✓	✓	✓
Stretching exercises	✓	✓	✓
Posture/ergonomic advice	✓	✓	✓
Progress reports	2	3	4
Rehab exercises	Basic	Corrective	Advanced
Lifestyle advice		✓	✓
Nutritional advice			✓
Injury prevention			✓
Optimum wellbeing			✓
Investment PAYG	£420	£630	£840
Block booking discount	£395	£595	£780

Complete Harmony

Treatment Packages

Using my experience, skill and knowledge each package has been created to bring about positive changes physical, mental and emotional. Your chosen package will be specially designed with your needs in mind.

Maintenance
This package is for you if you are looking for a monthly hour long treatment session to relax mentally and physical in order to maintain your emotional and physical health and well-being.

Rapid Response
This package is for you if you have had a major life changing experience. With the addition of massages this is package is designed to quickly reduce physical tension and bring about mental clarity and focus.

Relax, Re-focus & De-stress
This package is for you if you have been dealing with stressful situations and you are looking for some balance and focus in your life. If you want to feel more in control, uplifted and good about yourself then this package is for you.

	Maintenance 3 one hour sessions One session a month	Rapid Response 6 one hour sessions Two sessions a month	Relax, Re-focus & De-stress 9 one hour sessions One session a week
A specially selected Neal's Yard Remedies Organic gift package			✓
Reiki	✓	✓	✓
Reflexology (feet or facial)	✓	✓	✓
Reiki & reflexology	✓	✓	✓
Reiki or reflexology with a part-body massage		✓	✓
One head and a foot treatment		✓	✓
Metamorphic Technique		✓	✓
Relaxing guided visualisation recording		✓	✓
A journal to record your thoughts and feelings and map your progress		✓	✓
To help enhance this package bespoke lifestyle activities will be suggested			✓
Bespoke weekly worksheets			✓
A specially selected guided meditation recording			✓
Where appropriate crystals & essential oils will be incorporated into a treatment for their therapeutic benefits.			
	£135	£297	£459

Call Sharon Taylor on
07751 942234

sharon@complete-harmony.co.uk
www.complete-harmony.co.uk

Gain Customers in the Short - Term (3-6 months)

Develop a marketing strategy to implement over the next 3 to 6 months; create compelling reasons for customers to buy from you, gain more confidence with marketing to reap new and profitable business.

Light Bulb Marketing Methods

Use the light bulb rays to note down all the marketing methods you a) currently use and then b) can think of. This will spark ideas of what marketing methods you want to improve on *and* want to start utilising in order to create focused and considered actions and therefore results for your business.

Now extract the Top 5 actions from your initial marketing strategies:
(the 1st rule of marketing is to just get started)

More Marketing Ideas

You will start to notice that each marketing / content idea you have can be replicated across all your marketing channels. Just a few changes and tweaks to your overall message are required dependent upon the platform you are sharing it with.

Blog Posts
Blogging is an effective way of showcasing yourself as an expert in your field. Current Google rule of thumb for effective (2019) Search Engine Optimization (SEO) is in a 300-word blog mention your key word 5-7 times. Use these keywords in a way that feels natural and authentic. You can also use 1-2 long-tail key words – these are often question based key words that keep you on track for answering your ideal client's questions within your blog. So, 1st port of call – what are your key words? What your ideal clients typing in to google to find you or get the problem you can solve, solved?
What to write about: What issues do you solve for your clients? Common FAQs, Top 5 Tips for choosing to *use your services*, 'How to…'

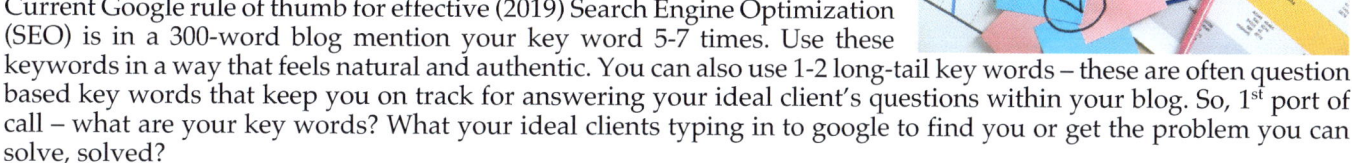

Freebies
Everybody enjoys something for free. What can you offer your potential ideal client that will help them get their initial questions answered and help them to see you as an expert? Think about what they need help in and provide a 'Useful guide to…' 'How to…' 'What to do when…' 'How to select your ideal *insert your business*' You can provide this information in any format of your choosing – a webinar, free download, audio file, a challenge and so on.

Social Media Campaign
Which social media platforms and tools suits you and your ideal customers best? Think about and plan for a campaign, to get you closer and in front of and interacting with your ideal clients. Which platforms do you know your ideal clients are hanging out on? For now, think about and action 5 posts to get them engaging. Test it. Social media is created to be sociable, so remember to engage and interact with people by commenting and liking.

E-Newsletter
Or a more attractive, appealing and fun name, for a way of keeping in touch with clients who love what you do! Either way whether you have 1 or 1001 on your list, it's important you keep at the forefront of your customers mind. Which newsletters do you love? What do you love about them: humorous, entertaining, informative, educative, sharing of tips, freebies? Create one for you and your crowd – these are a cheap and effective way to connect.

Your Website
Still by far the best and easiest tool to get you in front of your customers: get it right and working for you while you're not. Put yourself firmly in your ideal customers shoes and take a walk through your website, are you solving their issues, do you have testimonials, do all the links work, are the images relevant, where do you sit on Google ranking? See **Blog Posts** for good SEO ranking rules. It's worth getting yourself on a course to keep yourself up to date with SEO and Google as it changes so quickly.

Networking
Last year 70% of UK business was done via networking. With so many different groups out there: free, drop in, membership, formal, informal, large, small you'll find a group that suits you and your businesses needs. The key is consistency; go regularly and finding one where you can enjoy the people and the format. Find like-minded people and business will come naturally. Ask on social media for recommendations local to you. Step outside your comfort zone and try them out for size!

Go forth and Make it Happen!

Actions:

What 3 new actions will you take this month?

1. ……..

2. ……..

3. ……..

What results did you gain/heading towards? What did you learn?

How to write blog posts that get your business results

If you're a business owner wanting business growth through your website and via social media platforms a great way to do this is to write blogs. They offer a useful way to hone how you 'speak' with your audience and what message you share. Remember you can start with a blog and this can develop to a Vlog, a free download, an e-book and so on. No need to fear or be bored by the prospect of writing blogs. Here are some simple steps to get you off and writing!

Show off your Expertise

The first thing to do, before anything else, is to think about what challenges or problems your ideal client encounters. If you have completed your Ideal Client profile you already have this information. What key searches are they typing into Google? Jot down at least 12 problems they have. *See Magic Marketing* exercise. For example, as a beautician, your ideal client's problem might be 'How do I get clear skin?' So, your blog posts need to answer this issue: '5 ways in which to get clear skin' 'Best Tips for Clear Skin' 'Clear skin will attract your soul-mate!' (you get the picture!) and so on. That way you are solving your ideal clients' problems. What better way is there to show off your expertise?

Increase your SEO Search Engine Optimisation

If you want to get at the top of the page on Google searches, think about how your ideal client is finding you (see above). What terms are they inputting into Google to find you? Set up Google Analytics on your website to start tracking this information. Once you know this you can use those search terms and key words in your blog posts. Be sure to use it in your blog title and headers and within the body of the content. Use the term in a natural way that helps your client relate to the article and gain the information they need to learn more about their search.

Share your knowledge

To be the expert in your field, to be the go-to person for whatever product or service you provide it's important that you are generous with your knowledge. There is a saying in networking 'givers gain' and it's true. You are an expert in your field, so don't be afraid to give away your tricks of the trade, help people to help themselves first and then they are more likely to select you for your purchasable services.

Upload & Share

Choose an appropriate image to go with your post (see stock image sites) and now is the time to put your blog post on your website and put it out across your social media channels! You have got this.

Use this space to jot down your blog ideas

Setting 3-Month Goals

The clearer you are with your intentions and what you are aiming to achieve the more likely you are to get there. You can use this exercise to create some overall goals with your marketing. What do you want to achieve in the short term?

Goal/s:

Why do you want to achieve this? (the clearer you are with your why the easier it'll be to keep motivated)

Action Plan   Deadline

Action Plan   Deadline

Action Plan   Deadline

Your WHY is so important! It's your driving force. Why do you want to achieve these goals?

Gain Customers *Consistently*

Develop marketing strategies for the following 6-12 months - Create a consistent message to get you and your business in front of your ideal customers in the most cost and time effective way, to reap new and profitable business.

10 Actions to Achieve More of the same juiciness...

In business it's easy to get complacent with the business you win and forget the important bits, like *how* you are winning the business. I often hear business owners saying that they don't need to network or market anymore as they have all the business they need. This is complacency. Check out this exercise for you to focus on the HOWS, so you can keep getting more of what is currently working for you.

Thinking about your achievements and accomplishments in the last 12 months, if they felt good, what can you do to achieve more of the same? This is adapted from Esther and Jerry Hicks' book 'Getting into the Vortex'.

My accomplishments	How could I achieve more of the same?	What is my 1st step or action towards that?
Example: Winning a new client by successfully networking.	*Example: Attend more networking groups of a similar type.*	*Example: Research networking groups I want to attend that fit a similar profile to the one where I won new business*

Getting clear on your 12-Month Goals – Start with a plan of action

My 12 Month Focused Action Plan – What do you want to accomplish in the next 12 months?	What would you like to accomplish in the next 12 months?	What does this successful outcome look like?	What are your key questions around making this happen?	What strategies will you use to overcome your obstacles?	What will be your 1st action?	When will you complete this action?
1)						
2)						
3)						

NB: This is adapted from Fabienne Fredrickson's goal setting focus days.

Keeping in Touch (with your customers)

Working in a competitive (or any!) market it's important to keep one step ahead. It's all about creating 'Raving Fans'; customers who love what you do and will keep coming back to you time and time again.

In a world of information overload, it's time your message got to the top of their inbox, letterbox, in tray, social media feed. Here are a few ideas to get you started with effective ways to keep in touch with your customers:

Feedback Forms
Use feedback forms as part of your close with an existing customer - Ask 4 - 6 questions, i.e. how would they like to keep in contact, what other services would they find beneficial from you, what improvement/s would be beneficial to your service etc

Customer Survey
Use a free tool (Survey Monkey, Poll fish, Zoho) to create a survey to send to existing & previous for customers. Find out more about how you helped them, if you can help them further. What language do they use to talk about you?

Thank you, cards,
A great way of letting your customers knows they're loved, and their business appreciated. I send my customers a card in the New Year thanking them for their business in the previous year. Starts a new year in a positive way and puts my business at the forefront of their mind.

Be Sociable
Use social media to build trusting relationships. Shout about their knowledge and expertise, comment on their blogs, connect them with useful, strategic contacts of yours, and subscribe to their newsletters. Take an interest in them and the things important in their world.

Grab a Coffee. Keep abreast of what's going on
Whilst social media are great tools for keeping your customers up to date with what you're up to. Never underestimate the power of a coffee! Spend time finding out about them.

Event Invites
Keep up to date of what's going on locally to you - both for business and pleasure (networking, workshops) and suggest a meet up at event of mutual interest.

(**TIP:** I have a client who sent someone they really wanted to meet with a kettle and two cups, suggesting a meeting. Needless to say, it worked!)

Which idea will you start implementing?

Planning an E-Newsletter

There is still a place for email newsletters.
Whether you have a list of 1 or 1000 an e-newsletter can be developed with ease, efficiency and results. Follow these steps and your newsletter will be up and running in no time. Its time to get you at the forefront of your customers mind. Here's what you need to think about:

1) What you want to say?
Do you want to be informative, educative, entertaining, humorous etc.?

2) What do you want to achieve?
Give your audience a reason to engage with your brand. Do you want to create action, understanding, increase knowledge, a better click through rate to your website?

3) Have a clear call to action (C.T.A)
Find a reason to send your audience to your website. This will help with your SEO (Search Engine Optimisation) and build up brand awareness and engagement.

- ☐ Email me
- ☐ Buy this
- ☐ Read my blog
- ☐ Check out what my clients have achieved working with me

4) Select your FREE newsletter tool, i.e. Mailchimp, Sendblaster, Reachmail
All tools offer a free service up to a certain number of subscribers (usually around 1000) – find out which template and service works for you and your business.

5) Upload/Add your contacts
The tool you choose will give you instructions and is straightforward I promise! (NB Check GDPR rules around this)

6) Create your template
There is always lots of choice around this. Start with something simple. Remember to always use your own branding: images, logo, and common language. Make sure it reflects you and your business. Look at ones you're sent - what do you like and dislike and then model their approach.

7) Send it out to your audience
Start with monthly and always around the same time for consistency. Start with your existing clients and trusted network. Most importantly, be **consistent**.

8) Set Objectives and Track Results
A good place to start is 'Open Rate' and 'Click Rate'. You can compare to your industry (your provider will share this information) this gives you something to aim for each month, better results, more engagement etc.

9) Add a code to your website to gain 'Subscribers'
Your newsletter provider will give you a code to add to your website enabling your potential customers to easily sign up. Give away some fabulous freebies associated with your client's needs and this becomes easy.

Use this space to mind map your ideas and thoughts for your newsletter:

My Story- Your 'Why'

Sharing your 'why' really helps others to understand on an emotional level what it is you do and why it is you do it. People buy emotionally; therefore, your story can be hugely impactful.

"People don't buy what you do, they buy why you do it" says Simon Sinek, motivational speaker and organizational consultant, and author of five books, including; 'Start with Why'

Check out Simon Sinek 'Start with Why' video clip where he succinctly explains why you need to start with your why: www.youtube.com/watch?v=IPYeCltXpxw

Also read 'My Story' for ideas on how to approach *your story* (over on my website).
https://www.meta4coaching.co.uk/about-meta4/

You can use these four questions to prompt you into writing your story:

1) What challenges did you used to have? (Before you do what you do now?)

2) What steps did you take to help you overcome your challenges?

3) What difference has this made to your personal and professional life now?

4) What's your purpose now? (Who do you help and why?)

I leaped into the Unknown

Running a small business is a cinch…right? Resigning from a corporate career in early 2007 saw me embarking on running my own business. Even though my husband was self-employed, I went in completely naively, thinking that it was going to be easy, when in fact… I was always giving it my all – heart, mind and soul. At weekends always thinking of new ideas to bring in business and much needed money. Constantly mulling over what I wasn't doing and what I thought I should be doing. All this taking me mentally away from my family and friends and the fun stuff in my life, in exactly the same way as when I was in a JOB. The passion, the motivation and the enthusiasm I once had for running my own business was slowly but surely ebbing away. Ultimately, I knew, deep down and rationally, being a business owner and self-employed was what I wanted to pursue; I was good at coaching and the coaching clients I had, albeit very few, were getting great results and I thrived on seeing such positive changes happening for people and their lives. I started out as a Life Coach, wanting to hone my coaching skills before I utilised my corporate-life skills for businesses. I just didn't seem able to get enough coaching clients through the door to keep it a viable business.

Starting to make a real difference
I knew I was here to make a difference to my clients and to my family. I was learning on the fly and sometimes I made mistakes. I started to wonder if it wouldn't just be easier to get a job. Looking back I lacked clarity on my purpose, my offerings, the waters were getting muddied and I wondered: '…is this what's it's all about?'

On the verge of having to make some real tough decisions, I secured a training contract, training individuals with customer service and business admin skills. This was a lifeline. It provided a much-needed injection of cash and gave me the breathing space to work out what me and my business needed in order to move forward. In this time, I invested thousands of pounds in both business and personal development, working with a mentor. I started to integrate cutting edge trends, technology, and tactics for myself as well as my own clients. This simplified their experience, saving them both time and money which meant they see were seeing results quickly too.

So, in the years following 2007, I learned that running a small business was about simplifying. Simplifying what I offered and who I offered it to and how I shared my message. By 2010, 3 years in, I was finally attracting the clients I wanted to work with and knew I could make a difference with. I had structured coaching programmes, an attractive working website, a confident and clear business message and a positive mindset - all of which, when put together were the missing key ingredients for a successful small business.

Now, 13 years into my business I have financial freedom, I am motivated, confident and full of the right kind of focus and direction. I know the actions I take in my business for business development will reap continued success and the time I spend with my family and friends doing the fun stuff is balanced. It truly is life changing. I work with a coach and I know this is instrumental in making all the above happen.

7 Steps to a Successful Sale

It is a business fact that 48% of sales are NOT followed up. 48%!

These 7 simple steps are for business owners to follow and implement into your business, so you always deliver the same, great service and your prospects will ALWAYS be followed up with. You will have a clear process of how prospects are responded to and you will notice clear efficiencies occur when you implement these steps into the day-to-day running of your business.

A sale always starts with:

1) Marketing Activity (whether it's: Networking, Website, Social Media, Phone Call, and Letters etc.)

⇕

2) Attract Interest "I've spotted you through one of your marketing channels; I'm interested in what you do, tell me more..." = Can be a direct jump to step 4; however step 3 builds more trust. Engage your interested party: Showcase your Expertise/Offer help. Gain their contact details.

⇕

3) Connect with them on Social Media: LinkedIn, Twitter, like their business page

⇕

4) Speak to your interested party via **Email/Phone Call** Listen: Find out what they are looking to achieve (with your product/service).

⇕

5) Follow up by sharing your **Success Stories, Brochure** AND gain a small level of commitment by **asking them to answer 4 to 6 (Pre-qualifying) questions** to understand what they want to achieve. *See Kick Start Session Questions*

⇕

6) **Arrange a Meeting/Consultation** face to face or over the phone. Go through their Pre-qualifying questions, LISTEN, understand their needs and match them with what you offer. Clearly & confidently share your packages/services and investment.

⇕

7) **Close** - Have one (or two) tried & tested 'Double Bind' questions to help close the sale more confidently: *'If you were to go ahead, when would you like to get started, now or next week?'*

Write down your **7 Steps** to a Successful Sale:

Share your Expertise

Clearly recognise your key strengths and skills.
Establish the gaps to develop and build upon for your personal and professional growth.
Creating an understanding of these will help you to confidently share and sell your services.

Delegating and Prioritising

(taken and adapted from Gay Hendricks, The Big Leap)

Working out what you *love* to do and what you're *good* at doing will help you fully understand where your time is currently being spent versus where you want your time to *be* spent. The exercise will help you look more objectively at all the tasks you currently do to see which of them could be better placed elsewhere. Perhaps empowering a team member or finding someone else, a Virtual Assistant (VA) whose skills lie within that area of expertise. Use this exercise to note all the activities you have undertaken in your business in the last month or so and categorise them using this key: *See also *Favourite Subjects Matrix* to help you get started.

Zone of Incompetence – This is made up of all the activities you're not good at

Zone of Competence - These are the things you're competent at, but others can do them just as well.

Zone of Excellence – These are the tasks you do extremely well

Zone of Genius! – This is the set of activities you are uniquely suited to

Zone of Incompetence	Zone of Competence
Zone of Excellence	Zone of Genius

What actions / steps do you want to put in place to work more in your Zone of Genius?

e.g. Engage with a Virtual Assistant to take away the 'incompetence' tasks, create a specific service which helps me focus on my Zone of Genius.

My Favourite People – is an impactful exercise that will help you to understand *who* you thrive working with. Useful to gather more of those people around you. (These following 3 exercises are taken from, 'What Colour is your Parachute') Richard N. Bolles

Surround yourself with like-minded people

Column 1	Column 2	Column 3	Column 4
Places I have worked thus far	Kinds of people there who drove me nuts! (from the 1st column) Describe what was it about them that drove you nuts; e.g. bossy, late, left early etc.	Kinds of people I'd prefer not to have to work with, in order. (Ranking the items in Column 2 in exact order of which is worse)	Kinds of people I'd most like to work with, in order of preference. (The opposite of those qualities in the 3rd column, in the same order)

My Favourite Working Conditions – this exercise will help you understand *where* you thrive. Massively helpful for business owners to understand. I have come across many business owners who are getting stuck purely due to their work environment. Find out the *where* and the rest will follow.

	Column A Distasteful Working Conditions	Column B Ranked	Column C The Keys to My Effectiveness at work
Places I have worked thus far:	I have learned from the past that my effectiveness at work is decreased when I have worked under these conditions:	Among the factors or qualities listed in Column A, these are the ones I dislike absolutely the most (in order of decreasing dislike) 1 2 3 4 5 6 7 8 9 10	I believe my effectiveness would be at an absolute maximum, if I could work under these conditions (the opposite of the qualities in Column B - in order): 1 2 3 4 5 6 7 8 9 10

This exercise helps you to define where you thrive.

Favourite Subjects Matrix

	LOW	HIGH
Expertise	**4.** Subjects for which you have little enthusiasm and which you have little expertise	**2.** Subjects for which you have lots of enthusiasm but in which you have little expertise
	3. Subjects for which you have little enthusiasm but in which you have lots of expertise	**1.** Subjects you have lots of enthusiasm and which you have lots of expertise

Enthusiasm

Step 1: Use post it notes to jot down different subject fields within your business (or outside of!) and post them to the corresponding quadrant.

Step 2: Once done you are now clearer on your HIGH Enthusiasm and High Expertise subjects; list your subject areas here to keep you focused *and* to make sure you are utilising your skills to their fullest within your business:

1 _____
2 _____
3 _____
4 _____
5 _____
6 _____
7 _____
8 _____
9 _____
10 _____

Help yourself to stand out from the crowd. Recognise your strengths

Generate Referrals

Love the clients you have.
Keep your existing clients delighted so they will continue to buy from you and create an easy referral process.

Client Feedback Form

Asking your clients for feedback during and / or after they have finished working with you is essential for your personal and professional development. Hearing about the positive impact you and your service has had on your client is always going to be good to hear.

But more importantly, the not so good or improvements required is integral to *continued* business success. You are not always going to get it 100% right for every client every time. Here's how you find out what they loved and what they would love to see more of…

Ask for written testimonials - find out what else they would want to see from you to improve on your delivery.

Here's an example Feedback Form. Insert your specific business and services as appropriate. What do you want to find out?

Find out what your clients really loved about working with you…

Name:……………………………………………………………

What updates would you like to receive from me in the future?

Tick all that apply:

| Personal Development Workshops ☐ | 1-1 Coaching Opportunities ☐ |
| Business Growth Workshops ☐ | Business Networking Events ☐ |

How would you like to receive updates and keep touch? Tick all that apply:

Email ☐	LinkedIn ☐
Twitter ☐	Text ☐
Facebook ☐	Phone ☐

If you could suggest 3 improvements to your coaching experience what would they be?

1 _____

2 _____

3 _____

What other product or service offering would you find beneficial from me?

_____

Know of someone who would benefit from having a chat with me? Enter their contact details here. Make sure you have their permission first.

_____

Testimonials really help others with similar needs understand how they can benefit from coaching. Please share an enthusiastic expression of the benefits and results you have enjoyed from working together. This may be a helpful format for you to follow a) before working with me, (brief statement of your situation before) b) statement of the value you received c) The 3 most significant improvements (number of clients / results / income / outcomes / productivity, etc.)

Creating Referrals of a Lifetime

The following summary is extracted from the *'The Referral of a Lifetime'*, by Tim Templeton. I highly recommend you read it for a thorough understanding of a long-term business marketing strategy. It's a method I have been using in my coaching business for several years now and consistently each quarter send out an inspirational piece of marketing via the post to my referral partners*.

It's a long-term marketing strategy you can follow once you have clearly defined your ideal client. *Your Referral Partners are people in your network who are potentially ideal clients and/or can connect you with your ideal clients.

The marketing strategy is about keeping in **regular contact** with your ideal clients and educating people who you know, about the business you offer and the kind of clients you love to work with, so they can refer more of them to you. We all love to refer our friends and associates to great people so it's a win-win!

Be Authentic; Be You

It's important to embrace your uniqueness in business. This is what makes you stand out from the crowd, enables you to really love your business by engaging with the right clients and getting the best results for them. Check this table out to gain greater understanding of how you prefer to communicate, so your postal marketing continues to reflect you and your business.

Which communication type do you fit into?
(There is no one better than the other in business).
I've emboldened my approach.

Relational ………………….. Business	**Relational ………………….. Business**
Business ………………….. Relational	Business ………………….. Business

The 1st word represents how others see you in business relationships
The 2nd is your natural tendency in business relationships

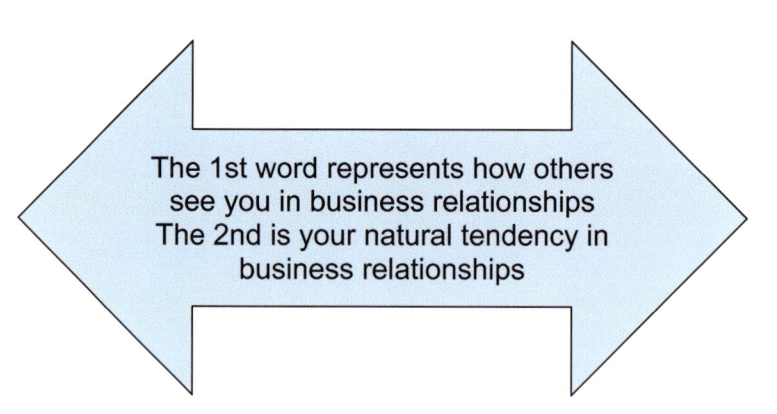

The 250 by 250 Rule

The business owners who network (and all should!) know, it's not who you know, but who your clients and associates know that matters. Start by combining a list of all the contacts you have; personal contacts, business contacts, current clients, past clients, anyone who you believe might be a fit for your products and services. Then reach out and ask them if they would like to become a Referral Partner. Share what you are aiming to achieve.

ABC your list – categorize to have a greater understanding of your list. Increase your awareness on what they will want to hear from you about.

A's: People who are your cheerleaders, they feel so strongly about you and your products and services that they would refer you right now. *Your A's are the ones most likely to refer you.*

B's: are individuals that you think can champion your cause as well as refer you if you educate them about how you work.

C's: individuals you are not sure about but still want to keep communicating with

Educate your list

Let them know what you do and how you work at regular and consistent intervals throughout the year.

1st step: send a letter telling everyone of your new business philosophy and proactive communication process – your relationship between you and your clients is your priority. By following this strategy, you can spend more time and money offering additional value to the clients you already serve. (see my template for 1st letter samples below.)

Put a 'contact regularly' system in place
Map out how you will communicate with your contacts for the next 12 months. Quarterly is a good start. Think about things that are going on in your business, what your contacts would find useful from you and what things are associated with you and your business for ideas and inspiration.

Your 'contact regularly' system might look something like this:

January – New Year card
April – Positive and inspiring quote card
September – Personalised newsletter
December – Christmas Greetings

Follow through on your contact strategy with consistency and authenticity with all your ABC's, adding to your list as you meet more people and watch your marketing and business soar!

Use this space to plan

Examples of Warm Letters, Introductory Letters & Cards

What can you send out to your network that will raise awareness of what you do, engage and inspire? Here's the 1st couple of letters that I sent out to over 100 of my connections to help you get started…

Clare Whalley
Meta4 Business Coaching Ltd
Brooks Rd
Sutton Coldfield
B72 1HP

Dear XXX

I hope this letter finds you and your family thriving. Recently I have taken the time to review my business and came to the decision to communicate more authentically and more frequently with the relationships I have developed to date.

So, to update you on where I'm at with my business; I'm happy to say my business coaching practice has grown into a solid and thriving business and my clients are raving about their results.

My ideal clients are start-ups and established business owners who want to make their money with more consistency and ease; working with more of the clients they love to work with and delivering the products and services they love to deliver. As you will know through our working relationship, clients go through a structured coaching programme and the results they receive help to create long term change and consistent results.

My client base is growing mostly through referrals. Would you please be on the lookout for friends or colleagues that currently need to focus on growing their business? I work with people all over the Midlands.

If you see a match, will you let them know about me and vice versa? I'd love a chat with them to see if I could help. Alternatively, they can call me with any questions on 07739 196896 or visit my website at www.meta4coaching.co.uk If I'm not the right coach however, I have many colleagues who may be better suited and will be happy to refer them.

Thanks for your help! If there's anything I can do my end to help you, in any capacity, please let me know. It would be great to meet up for a coffee soon, let me know your availability.

Till then,

Clare

Clare Whalley
Meta4 Business Coaching Ltd
Brooks Rd
Sutton Coldfield
B72 1HP

Dear XXX

I hope this letter finds you and your family thriving. I'm starting to change how I keep in touch, so it's more authentic. I'd love to hear about what you're up to and working on, both personally and professionally. To start off as I intend, here's what's new with me:

On a personal note:

- Isabelle has just started year 1 after very happy end to her reception year at school. She's doing brilliantly and loves every new school day. Long may it last!
- James is 20 months and is now walking and bumping into everything and everyone and is also trying out his first few words.
- We've just been on a 17-day road trip in an RV around the Midwest states. 4 adults and 3 children in a 32-foot campervan, it was brilliant and very tiring!
- Have just booked into the Birmingham half marathon – the furthest I've ever run. A client challenged me to it so how could I say no?

On a professional note:

- I'm continuing coaching business owners; helping them to grow businesses they love, and I am recently basking in my client success of expanding her team in her beautiful new chiropractic practice.
- Since February I have been on the executive committee for the Sutton Coldfield Chamber of Commerce and I am enjoying having a voice in my hometown seeing how we can help small businesses achieve more from their local area.
- A roll out of leadership and management courses to a Birmingham-based company delivering communication skills, team motivation and dealing with conflict has been transformational!

My client base is growing steadily through referrals, for which I'm really honoured. If you see a match will you let me know about them and vice versa? I would love to have a chat with them to see if I could help.

Looking forward to connecting more frequently in hearing what's new with you, too. It would be great to meet up for a coffee, let me know when would be good for you.

All my best,

Clare

> Think of imaginative ways of grabbing your referral partner's attention!

THE MOOSE OF MOTIVATION

- A journey of a thousand miles begins with a single step
- Turn your dreams into plans
- Don't make excuses, make progress

Happy New Year!
Here's to a prosperous and successful year ahead!
I hope you're able to look back on 2016 with good memories
of achieving most (if not all!) of what you set out to…

The great thing about January is new starts.
Take the time to think about how you will
make the most of your 2017.

Best wishes for a wonderful year ahead,

Clare

"Obstacles are those frightful things you see when you take your eyes off your goal" Henry Ford

Case Studies

Case Studies are a great way of cementing your knowledge and understanding around what a client has got out of working with you and why they chose to work with you in the first place. Put all the relevant details together on the process you both went through and these steps will help others in a similar position understand what they can get out of working with you too. Start sharing this across your social media channels (LinkedIn is a great start) and your website. Here is a simple format to follow with the main headlines you may wish to address:

Create a clear title (in line with what your ideal clients are looking to achieve with you)

'Gain more clients; make more money.'

Client Background

Maxine booked a block of business coaching sessions as she'd lost focus in her business of 18 months and confidence in herself. She was looking to regain her focus and make her business as successful as she had once believed it to be. This is what Maxine was aiming for:

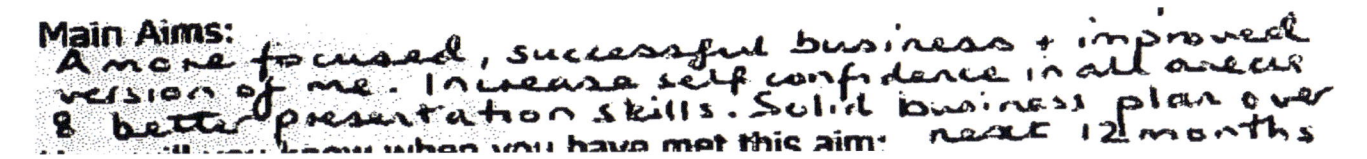

> **Main Aims:** A more focused, successful business + improved version of me. Increase self confidence in all areas & better presentation skills. Solid business plan over next 12 months

Steps

The first step was to put a coaching programme together based on Maxine's main aims. The programme covered 5 x 2-hour sessions, so Maxine could start to see and feel instant results. The 1st session included some NLP (Neuro-linguistic programming) techniques to help present herself as a confident, professional & trustworthy businesswoman when networking and meeting potential clients. Then it was time to perfect the delivery and content of a short business presentation in line with her short-term goals.

Goal setting is essential to any business growth programme. Establishing where you are now and where you want to get to, ensures focus in the right areas. In Maxine's business it helped to do this by working out what her desired monthly financial return was and more importantly how she wanted to run her week, what business she wanted to be doing and from where. From this point we were able to establish the steps she could take in order to get her there; a focussed marketing campaign, her own clinic where Maxine would spend 2 days per month – building up to 1 day a week, networking and speaker slots, contacts who could help her, to name a few of the steps.

> *Writing case studies of your work and how it has helped people who have worked with you is an easy way to share how others in similar positions can also achieve great results. Here is a simple outline.*

Then it was all about taking action. What were the first steps she could take, checking what resources and skills she needed along the way? Eating the elephant one small bite at a time!

Throughout the coaching programme it's important to assess what steps are working and what steps need tweaking and if there are any further resources, tools needed in order to achieve.

Outcome

Maxine now regularly attends networking groups within her clinic radius, she is obtaining referrals leading to client work, and she has and still is negotiating strategic alliances with local business owners and is looking into what other businesses will work well being aligned. Maxine has launched 'Maximise You', one of her main goals - her own clinic room in South Birmingham; which through the introduction of a monthly newsletter, as a way of keeping in touch with her existing client base, has been full in recent months. Here's what Maxine now says of her business:

'I'm so glad I met Clare. She is professional, reliable & extremely good at Life/Business Coaching. She was able to quickly understand my current business situation, to fixate on areas I was lacking, including my confidence & self-perception, to enable me to realise my business potential. She is very structured in her approach and throughout the coaching sessions, I felt a more successful and pro-active version of myself by the finish!' Maxine Moseley

Develop a Positive Mindset

A positive mindset is key for business success and not to be underestimated.
Here are some strategies for developing a positive and successful mindset to enable you to work in your business with an achieving attitude for you to reap successful outcomes on all the actions you take.

Accomplishment List (My TaDa's)

Name: ……………………………………

Ever since the day you were born (which was a great day!) you have been goal setting and achieving. Quite probably without realising it. On a day-to-day basis it easy to fall into work mode and ignore all that we've accomplished. Make a list of all the wonderful things you have done, all the great things you have achieved. This is your 'Accomplishment' or 'Ta-Da!' list.

Whichever way you choose to approach it, always note down your achievements! That way it's easier to replicate in the future.

As you write down your achievements think about which area of your life you achieved them in:

Discovery & Adventure (D&A), Family & Relationships (F&R), Fitness & Wellbeing (F&W), Giving Back (GB), Learning & Growth (L&G), Work & Finance (W&F) add these areas to your list to reveal how balanced your achievements are.

Date	My accomplishments	Area

Money Mindset and Beliefs
(Taken from Deb Golec's 'Papillion Coaching')

A common trait across business owners are limiting beliefs around money. Limiting beliefs around your financial self-worth and what you can potentially earn running your own business. This is a great exercise to do if you feel it would be helpful for you to think more positively about money. Follow the prompting questions and write down your 1st thoughts…

So many money blocks are locked in due to parental beliefs. Time to release them!

My mother felt money was…

My father felt money was…

What I observed with regards to money was…

I was always told that money…

My own early experience with money…

I'd love to earn more money, but…

In order to have more money, I'd need to…

I'm afraid if I had more money I would…

Having more money will make me…

My friends and family will think that…

Now create a positive money affirmation / mantra (start in the here and now: I am…)
What do you want to *think* about money, how do you want to *feel* about money? What do you want to start seeing where money is concerned? Make it as visceral as possible. This is your starting point.

The affirmation is such an important step in starting to address the negative belief and install a more positive, useful way of thinking about money and what you *can* achieve.

I am…

Write your positive money affirmation down and practice until you start feeling its truth.

Urgent & Important Matrix

Being able to prioritise and focus on business development tasks as well as client delivery work is key to you gaining more control of your business and put you in the driving seat. A useful way of planning your tasks is to use this "Urgent and Important Matrix". (Adapted from '7 Habits of Highly Effective People' by Stephen R Covey)

At the end of the process you will be able to devise action plans to work more effectively within the **important and non-urgent** space. The purpose of tackling the important and non-urgent tasks first is to ensure that they don't become important and urgent. If you find you are spending all your time on **urgent** *and* **important** tasks you are constantly firefighting – this is stressful and not conductive to a long-term business strategy.

You will work more effectively in your business if you become more proactive rather than working reactively = less stress, more productivity.

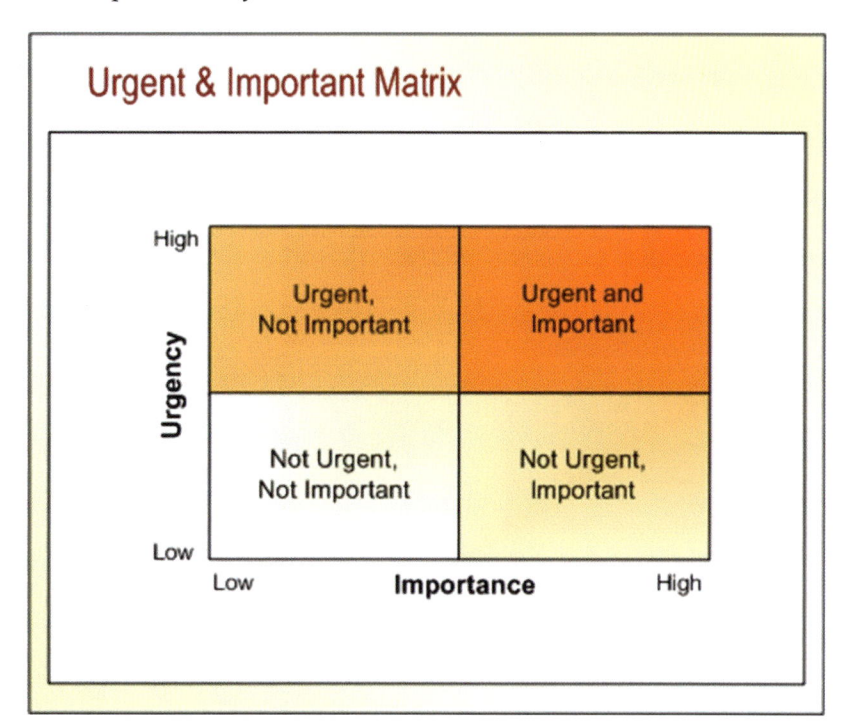

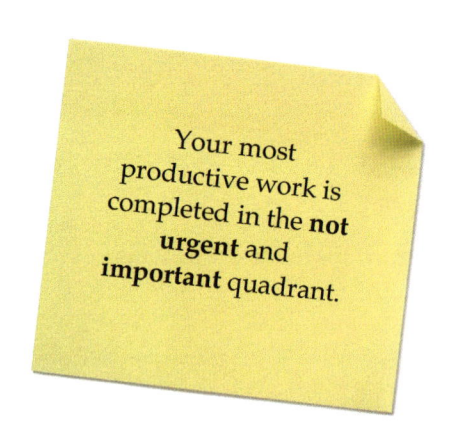

Urgent & Important Matrix

	Low Importance	High Importance
High Urgency	Urgent, Not Important	Urgent and Important
Low Urgency	Not Urgent, Not Important	Not Urgent, Important

*Your most productive work is completed in the **not urgent** and **important** quadrant.*

Tip - Start by writing down all the tasks you would like / need to get done over the next two weeks to one month. Write each of them down on a post it note and place in the corresponding quadrant.

It's useful to also note how long you believe each task will take you to complete. This takes away the overwhelm, helps you to manage your time more realistically and enables you to chunk down / make smaller the tasks. Use the Daily Accountability Sheet (on the next page) to manage your day more effectively.

When eating an elephant, take one bite at a time'
Creighton Abrams

Daily Accountability Sheet

This is your daily accountability sheet. Use it as a prompt so you can focus **on** daily business development actions as well as working **in** your business.

It stops the day taking control of you so you can be more in control of your day.

Do this activity before switching on your laptop - takes 2-3 minutes and you can focus on tasks that take 5 minutes to complete to several hours, dependent upon your day.

Keep remembering **WHY** you are striving for your end goal too, that will help to keep your motivated and inspired.

What 3 things can you do today that will get you closer to your big goals (These will be your priorities for your day). Be realistic and bold too.

1)

2)

3)

Name your biggest potential time-wasting activity today and write down what you can do to avoid it.

Dump it. Delegate it. Deal with it!
Weekly Planner – an additional way of planning your time and tasks

• Week Commencing: ……………………………………...

Planning for the week ahead will help you complete all Important / Not urgent (II) activities before they become Urgent and Important

• Including professional and personal activities will give you balance

• Establish which quadrant below your activity is in; you will start to gain organisation and calm across all areas

Be more productive. Find ways that help you achieve your to-do list, i.e. switch phone to silent, shut down email, put your timer on for specific tasks etc.

Urgent	Not Urgent
I Activities: Crises, Pressing Problems, Deadline driven projects	II Activities: Prevention ¨Recognising new opportunities ¨Planning¨ recreation¨ relationship blog
III Activities: Interruptions, some calls, some emails, some meetings	IV Activities: Trivia, busy work, some mail, some calls, time

Activity	Personal	Professional	Quadrant No.	✓

Develop Confidence & Self Belief

Achieve more of what you want with increased confidence and self-belief.
Effective tools to use in a variety of situations to develop a more confident and in control you.

Accomplishments this year

It's easy, leading a busy life, and as business owner to set goals and when you achieve them to move on to the next goal without taking stock and recognising what you've achieved.

Before you start to set goals for the next year, first let's recognise what you achieved this year in your personal and professional life and take a moment to think about *how* it was achieved; confident delivery, experience, new skills or knowledge, a useful connection etc.

Use this sheet to document and recognise your accomplishments as you go...

Wall of Success
A great way to note your achievements is to create a 'wall of success.' You'll need: flipchart paper & pen. Build a brick each time you accomplish and write the achievement in each brick.

My accomplishment:	How I did it:

Positive Self Image

This is an amazingly powerful exercise that will help you achieve feelings of an intense confidence boost and transformation. Follow the steps and give it the time and space it deserves for your injection of confidence.

> *You'll need a partner for this exercise. Grab a trusted friend to run through the script for a more confident and 'in-control' you.*

First, when you think of *presenting or walking into a packed room* insert desired outcome. Where are you on the Self Image O-meter scale? (See next page)

- **Self Image O-meter**

Nearly everyone has criticisms about them self or self-image; some people just hide it better than others!!

- **What do you see when you think about that? And what else...and what else...? (Jot down the negatives 1)**

- **Time to turn the negative list into positive statements, starting 'I am…' and repeat in a strong, firm, bold voice. Look towards your end goal – what are you aiming to achieve?**

Think of someone really (*insert required state*) *Confident*

Imagine (*insert name*) standing in front of you. Step into (*insert name*)

How does he/she feel?

What is he/she wearing?

What is her/his internal dialogue; i.e. what is he/she saying?

Where in the body does he/she feel it?

Give that feeling a colour and move it to where he/she feels good. Move the colour and push it from top to bottom. Increase the brightness and double it again.

Staying in this person's perspective, open your eyes, what do you see/feel?

- **Self Image O-meter – where are you on the scale now? (Chart on the next page)**

Remember a time when someone paid you a compliment. Close your eyes and relive the compliment. Hear what they said and see what you saw at that time. Re-live the feelings you felt when you heard the compliment. If it helps make the colours rich, bright and bold – push it from top to toe.

- **Self Image O-meter - where are you on the scale now? (Chart on the next page)**

Close your eyes – imagine someone in front of you who loves and respects you. Float out of your body and into theirs – look at yourself from their eyes. Hear what they say and see. Make the colours rich, bright and bold – push it from top to toe.

- **Self Image O-meter - where are you on the scale now? (Chart on the next page)**

Self Image O-Meter

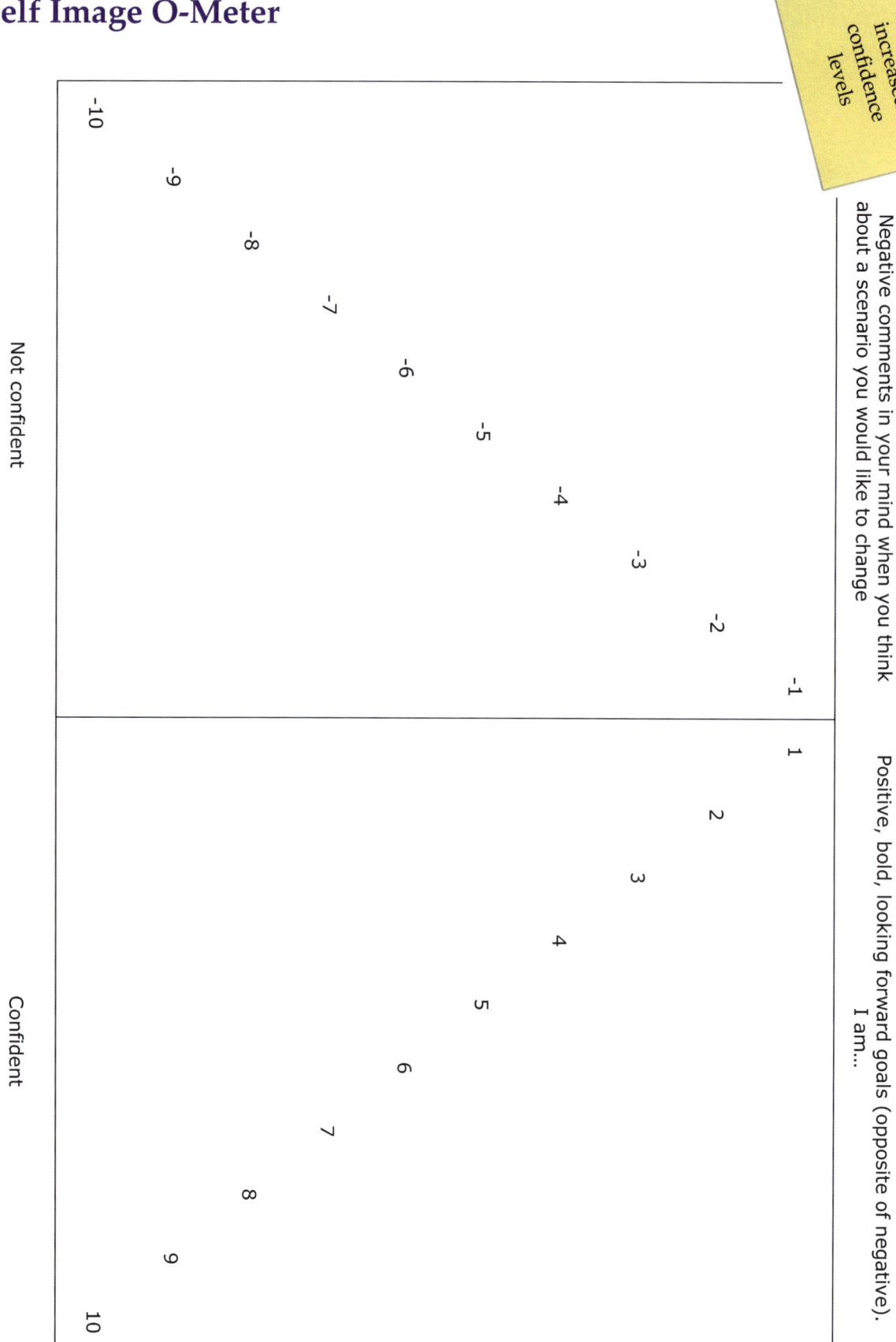

Use this scale to chart your increased confidence levels

Negative comments in your mind when you think about a scenario you would like to change

Positive, bold, looking forward goals (opposite of negative). I am....

Not confident

Confident

-10, -9, -8, -7, -6, -5, -4, -3, -2, -1

1, 2, 3, 4, 5, 6, 7, 8, 9, 10

Boost Your Confidence

Confidence is a learned skill, or at least it can be if you want to learn it!

In NLP (Neuro-Linguistic Programming) there are some useful and easy to implement tools and techniques. Here is another of my favourites to get you in to a positive, confident state of mind.

#Tip: Read through the steps a couple of times first.
#Tip: Find yourself a quiet space and 10 minutes to spare

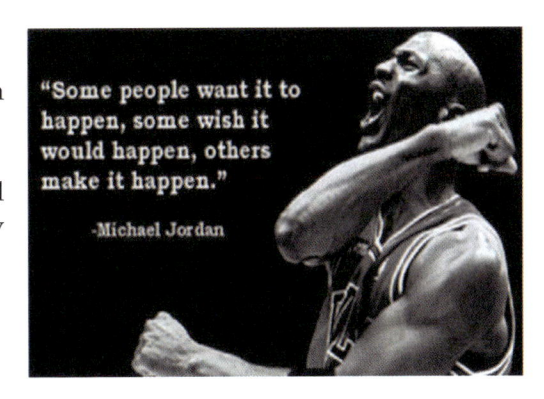

> "Some people want it to happen, some wish it would happen, others make it happen."
>
> -Michael Jordan

This NLP technique is called 'Anchoring' it's about placing a positive feeling or emotion to somewhere physically on your body. I use the classic yoga pose for this; however, you can use index finger and thumb, finger on a knuckle etc.

1) Firstly, remember a time in your life when you have felt confident. This could be, good at cooking lasagne, on your wedding day, on holiday.

2) Then place yourself back in this moment and create a vivid picture, as vivid as you possibly can. Make all the colours in the picture are bright and bold. Hear everything you heard at that time. Remember exactly *how* you felt and *where* (in your body) you felt it.

3) Then, when your feeling is at its peak attach to your anchor. Hold the pose until the confident, positive feeling starts to lessen. (The purpose of the anchor is that you can access this confident feeling wherever and whenever you need it, and nobody will know!

4) Think about something entirely different. What are you having for your tea tonight?

5) Finally test it. Re-attach to your anchor (your pose). What feelings come back? Do you feel more confident, in control?

#Tip: It's especially useful to 'attach' an uplifting piece of music to this too. What song do you love to sing along to? What song always gets you moving? Listen to the song, whilst reflecting on the good, confident memory.

#Tip: Practice your anchor. Get the feeling to the point as soon as you hear that piece of music or attach to your anchor you feel great. Use it when you need it. You will really notice the difference, I promise!

Notes

Share Clear Messages

Being able to develop and deliver a business presentation to share your compelling message is integral to your business success. Become an expert in your field and create positive revenue generating results.

Developing a 60 Second Business Presentation

So much business in the UK (and the world) is done via networking, over 70%. Face to face networking is a great way to meet like-minded business owners, share ideas and challenges and learn new tools beneficial to your small business development.

It can also be a daunting experience for many business owners. Worth remembering that confidence is a learned skill and the more you do it, the easier it becomes. And remember everyone in the room is just like you or they have been where you are at some point in their business journey. *See Confidence Building exercises*

Be prepared with your elevator speech.
An elevator speech is a clear, brief message or "commercial" about you. It communicates who you are, what you're looking for and how you can benefit a company or organization. It's typically around 30- 60 seconds, the time it takes people to ride from the top to the bottom of a building in an elevator.

Here is my 60 Second Business Presentation. I change it slightly each month, dependent upon a) the audience, b) what elements of my offering I want to focus on c) Props I may use:

Hi, my name is Clare Whalley and my business is Meta4 Business Coaching. I have been working as a Business Coach since 2007.

I help small business owners gain more clarity, focus and direction to achieving their goals.

I do this by coaching ambitious business owners through structured 12-month coaching programmes that provide guided solutions to all the key business growth challenges, with clear resources so they can achieve their desired results.

I offer a free business kick start session. If you would like to gain more clarity, focus and direction in your business, you can book in on my website www.meta4coaching.co.uk.

Here are the important elements of an elevator speech / short business presentation to practice yours:

Hi, my name is:

My Business is:

I help people achieve....

I do this by…

Name, Business Name

Top 10 Tips for Presenting

1 - Be yourself - Your audience wants to see YOU!
Remember people buy from people. It's cliché, but true.

2 - A small amount of nerves is good
Under pressure your body gives off a chemical, which naturally helps you think on your feet. Learn to embrace this feeling.

3 - Presenting is a 'Learned Skill'
So, you MUST practice in front of a mirror, trusted friend/colleague, video camera etc.

Presenting is a learned skill. Once you have it, you can achieve much more. Here are some tips for starters...

4 - Get your audience involved
Ask questions, include pair/group work. Ensures they are listening, get engaged in the presentation and helps you to relax and enjoy it.

5 - Memorise your introduction
Inside out and back to front. This creates a more confident and in control impression of you, thus helping you to relax from the start.

6 - If you make a mistake your audience doesn't need to know
Take a moment to re-compose, pause and carry on – it's likely your audience won't have even noticed.

7 Know your audience
Use humour, facts and knowledge appropriately.

8 - Have an Objective
What do you want as a result of the presentation? Have one objective and this will keep you focused and on track for what you want to achieve.

9 - Be comfortable with your topic
Only present on subjects you understand and believe in - you persuade people with passion.

10 - Practice, Practice, Practice!

Notes:

Top 10 Tips for Being a Great Networker

Statistics show us that a whopping 70%+ of business done in the UK (in 2017) was done via networking. Embrace networking and it will continue to boost your business as well as taking away the loneliness of being a business owner. You'll learn lots and continue to meet new people.

#1   The more you give the more you get back. Get involved as much as you can.

#2   Book 1-1's with members and **LISTEN** to understand others business.

#3   Plan and prepare your 60 seconds: Who are you? What do you offer? What referrals and contacts are useful for you?

#4   Be prepared to share ideas - be open to different ways to tackle business challenges and issues.

#5   Ask questions in 1-1's - the best way to find out about each other is to ask, 'how we can help one another?'

#6   Commit to attending: If it's a regular, membership type networking group - send a substitute to represent your business for the meetings you're unable to attend. Show consistency and reliability, good business sense.

#7   Remember People buy **YOU** - Networking is supposed to be fun and friendly! Find a group that meets all your needs!

#8   Share what makes you and your business unique. Aim to stand out.

#9   Make personal connections; leads to great recommendations and joint ventures.

#10 Use a hook in your 60 seconds - a tip, a 'prop', a visual, to help people remember you and your business.

Use this space to develop your own 60-second business presentation. Include your name, your business, and what you offer. Remember, Einstein said, 'If you can't explain it to a 6 year old, you don't understand it yourself.' Check out the video on my About Me page - https://meta4coaching.co.uk/about-us/ to develop your ideas.

Case Study - 'Develop a scalable business; more focused implementation'

You can also share excerpts from your case studies in your 60 seconds and business presentations to share more information on how your products and services have helped others…

Client Background
Lisa has been running her Chiropractic business for 5 years. Lisa is an ambitious small business owner with many personal and professional goals; she was ready to relocate locally and build her business to have a team of chiropractic assistants, employ another chiropractor, develop her communications skills to promote and market her business confidently and increase her weekly chiropractic guests by 40% with a matching financial increase. Lisa's overall mission:

> "My mission for coaching over the next 12 months is to remove any barriers to my success and happiness and to grow my business so that it can function without me."

Steps Lisa took:
Lisa identified specifically what she wanted to achieve for herself and her business for the forthcoming 12 months. Developing a detailed statement of all her desired business outcomes. Following a structured coaching programme, we firstly focused on areas that were proving to be barriers to her success, confidence, clear direction and limiting beliefs. Lisa was then able to focus on developing a clear and definitive vision for her rebranded business, a clear sales process and the best products and services to ensure her chiropractic guests health and wellbeing needs are always being met and exceeded.

Outcome and Results
18 months on, Lisa has 2 chiropractic assistants, a rebranded and relocated business, renewed freshness, vigour, confidence and motivation. She has a clear and definite business offering in the form of health packages that her chiropractic guests can easily identify themselves with. She has achieved her 40% increase in weekly guests on a consistent basis. She markets her business successfully through regular spinal screens and is now in the process of building a beautiful garden room to accommodate an additional chiropractor who can work alongside her and when Lisa is away, so Zest's guests can always be looked after.

Another great way to reflect on a service you have delivered and the impact it has had. Sharing stories is a great marketing tool. How can you use case studies to enhance your business message?

What Lisa says about her business now...

"Coaching with Clare has really helped transform my business to one that I am proud of and love being part of. Clare helped me understand & work on the things that were holding me back to allow the changes to begin…offering sound, constructive advice and tough love when I have definitely needed it! Our structured sessions have helped me achieve many things including re-branding my business, moving premises, having an open day party, changing my fees and introducing a membership scheme. My marketing plan is much improved and I am much clearer on how to get the best from things by setting a positive intention. I totally recommend Clare to anyone who needs to understand & overcome their business or personal challenges"

Selling Made Easy

Create a replicable process from your prospects' initial interest through to closing the sale. Create an engaging and authentic customer experience.

Top 10 Tips to a Sustainable & Successful Business

1 - Keep in contact with previous customers/clients
Via social media, free check-ups, sending memorable souvenirs or thoughtful gifts.

2 - Know, & keep in close contact with the people who can help you expand/build your business
Attend local networking groups, online groups, set up a trusted coaching or mastermind group, keep connected with previous clients.

3 - Offer something free to your potential customer base
Top Tips via your website, open surgeries, free consultations.

4 - Offer better customer service than your competition!
Give your customers a reason to always come back to you. What value can you add to your existing service that is compelling and exciting?

5 - Reward customers/clients who refer business to you
A small discount off future products/services, a gift out of the blue.

6 - Spend at least 10% of your working week developing your business
Via social media, blogging, setting goals, writing good engaging shareable content.

7 - Make sure all your promotional materials are professional, fresh and matches your company branding
What impression do your website, business cards, brochures etc. give? Take an objective viewpoint. Ask trusted others for feedback.

8 - Always set business goals for the next 12 months
Write them down, make them SMART, attach visuals to them and place somewhere prominent. Keep referring to them and checking in.

9 - Be clear where your current clients are coming from, or where you would like them to come from
A traffic lighted spreadsheet is useful to understand this, cost versus return on your marketing resources.

10 - Enjoy, take pride and have passion in what you do!
Your enthusiasm will shout out to your customers. Enthusiasm is infectious!

Notes:

Kick Start Business Pre-Qualifying Questions

This is 'Step 5' of the '7 Steps to a Successful Sale.'

These questions will help you to qualify your prospect. They will help your potential client to understand more about what you can offer them. It also helps you stand out from the crowd, by getting more of an understanding of what they are looking to achieve with your services. It's a win-win.

Here's an example of the types of question you may wish to ask.

What do you want to know from your potential client? Adapt the questions to fit in with your business and your clients.

Business Name………………..…………………………………

In which month & year did you start your business? …………

Your Top 3 reasons for creating your business:

1)

2)

3)

What are your top 3 business challenges?

1)

2)

3)

Being as S.M.A.R.T as you can (Specific, Measurable, Achievable, Realistic, Timed); list 3 **short-term** goals you would like to work on in the next 3 months.

1)

2)

3)

Which of those goals would you like to start working on 1st?

Where do you see you and your business in 12 months' time?

If you could solve these challenges, how much would this be worth to you over the course of your lifetime?

What would you like to see as a result of working with a coach?

Additional Notes:

> Creating a set of questions for a potential client to answer before meeting with you makes the sale easier. They will feel more committed & you will understand their challenges better.

Top 10 Mistakes to Avoid in your Job when Planning your Start-up

#1 Don't tell your boss! That's obvious - hopefully! No matter how pally you are with your boss keep your start-up plans to yourself. Redundancy, pay rises, could come up during the planning stages and you wouldn't want to miss out.

#2 Don't share your start-up idea with all and sundry. There will always be naysayers. People love to tell you why it won't work. It's time to start surrounding yourself with positive, like-minded, ambitious people, who are ready to support you.

#3 Don't think it's going to be easy There is no such thing as an overnight success. Behind every successful business is a business owner who is dedicated, committed, goal oriented and tenacious and who really has put the time in to get out what they want.

#4 Don't give up your job without a clue as to your starting point. (OK, you can, but it's so much easier if you seek some help first). There are so many people out there who can help guide you and create a plan with you to give you clarity: a mentor, business coach, Prince's Trust etc. Give yourself some breathing space to work out your 1st and 2nd steps.

#5 Don't think too far in advance. Yes, it's important for you to know what you want from your business; what it's going to look like and what you want it to deliver for you. But, more importantly it's about you taking that first small step forward, one step at a time.

#6 Don't have misguided loyalty. Be loyal to yourself 1st and foremost. Protect your own interests.

#7 Don't waste any time. Use up any holiday allowance going on courses, networking, exhibitions, events - anything that is going to help you develop personally and professionally for your new start up.

#8 Don't assume your company will look after your interests when you leave your job. Make sure you have any outstanding bonuses, paid holiday, pension, share schemes all wrapped up and you understand the implications if (when!) you leave. Your HR department (or an independent one) will confidentially deal with any questions you have. Get anything important in writing. I learnt this the hard way.

#9 Don't burn any bridges. You never know who in the current job will come in useful in the future. We all take different paths, so leave with your dignity and professionalism intact!

#10 Save some money. Whilst you're earning, save as much as you can. 10% is a great rule to follow and you will be so grateful and pleased with yourself when you leave and have money in the bank to get started: business cards, website, networking groups will be at the top of your investment list!

Notes:

Start-Up Business Checklist

Some people are under the illusion that when you start a business everything has to be perfect, attempting to attain what an established business would have worked years to achieve: premises, staff, beautiful stationery, big named customers on their 'order book'.

Here's a more realistic tick list of what you need in order to deliver a service led business to your customers.

☐ **A Business Name** - this can prove to be quite a challenge, especially if you consider yourself to be not that creative. Mind Map all the words and phrases you like and all the colours you believe would fit the most. Let all this ferment and the ideas and answers will start to flow. Share when you're ready with trusted people, those who have been down the path you are heading down.

☐ **Confidence and Self-Belief** - may seem like an odd one to put down on this checklist as it's an intangible. It is so important, even more so than the tangibles. If others do not feel you have the confidence in your ability, product, service then they just won't buy from you. (See 'Boost Your Confidence')

☐ **A Product or Service** - Obvious right? Be your customer for a minute, step outside of you and your new start-up. Is there a product or service with tangible results that your customers would love to easily purchase?

☐ **Marketing Material** - From a Facebook page to a Twitter account and business cards to a fully-fledged website. Your business at the start-up stage does not have to be all singing all dancing. It does, however, need to present a professional image with clear call to actions, i.e. can your potential customers easily get in touch with to find out more or buy from you from the outset?

With these items checked off you're ready to market and promote you and your business!

Notes for your start-up checklist:

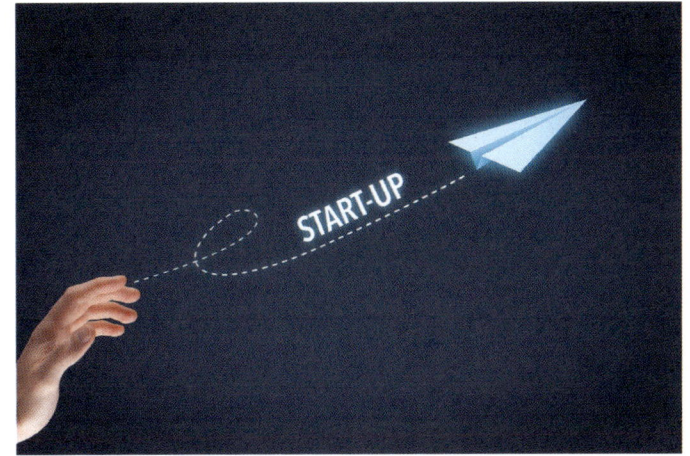

Beginner's Guide to Starting a Business in 3 Hours Per Week

3 hours doesn't sound a lot, but over just one month that equates to nearly 2 solid days of dedicated start-up focus. Manage your start-up time well, working in solid chunks and you'll be amazed at the progress you will be making.

Some examples of a month's worth of 3 hour time blocks:

Mind Mapping
Mind Map all ideas for your future business. No filter; write down everything you know about your start-up. Then look at the *how*, break down your goals and targets into smaller month on month actions. Ask yourself questions like "How will I get closer to achieving that?" and, "What are the options available to me?"

Create Your Offering
The single most important piece of work you can do for your start-up is asking and answering this question: 'What will my customers buy from me?' Make it as easy as possible for your customers to do business with you. Package up an offering, give your potential customers 3 choices, add value to your packages, make it easy and clear as to what benefits your customers will receive when buying from you, what problems will you be solving, e.g. helping people to become more organised and less stressed, helping business owners create socially engaging media content, build more profitable relationships etc.

Identify your Ideal Customer
Once you have your packages/offering sorted whom do you want to be selling to, working with? At this stage it's all about your ideal (as any business should be) what do you know about them already age, gender, demographic, geographic, challenges etc.? Then ask yourself where they hang out, where are you most likely to find them: Facebook, LinkedIn, Twitter, networking events, local groups. Do lots of research around this. What are they concerned with, what keeps them awake at night how would they like to get this problem solved?

Networking & Local Events
Find out about all the local business events happening near you. You'll be amazed at the sheer amount of local business-related events there are. You will have the opportunity to network, share ideas, challenges, uncover other business opportunities. You don't need to be a business owner to do this. There is loads of support available.

Notes:

The 5 Most Important Investments to Make in your Start-Up Business

When you are just starting out in business it's very easy to get distracted by new and shiny items for your start-up and get duped into investing heavily from the outset in things that are unnecessary. If you're offering a service led business (rather than product based) your initial outlay can be streamlined into the following investments:

A website that works

Often the most challenging of purchases to any new business owner, if you have little to no experience of web design, where do you start? Firstly, what do you know about your start-up business values, culture, what do you stand for - write down what colours, language and images that reflect your world. Next, do your research, look at others in similar fields to you; what will make your start-up stand up to your competitors *AND* stand out from your competitors? Remember your website is your shop window, it not only needs to be found but once found encouraging people to find out more and buy into you. Your website is an investment that needs to grow and develop as you, your business and the market does and is a worthy start-up investment and can be done well for less than £1000 for the year.

Business Branding

These top two go hand in hand. Make sure your logo, business name and colours reflect your start-up business identity. The values exercise is your starting point. Once you have a clear business identity in place, your marketing message and whom you're aiming to attract will work together. You are aiming to reflect a professional, here-to-stay, expert image to your ideal customers and unless you have experience in design, develop your branding with an expert in their field and it will be an investment that will return over and over for the lifetime of your business.

Hire A Business Coach

20% of small businesses are now using a Business Coach to grow their business and 79% of medium to large businesses. For start-ups, hiring a business coach will help you to plan and execute your plan in the best way possible for more successful short and longer-term results. Not only will a business coach keep your accountable for those successful results they will keep you motivated and inspired and help you develop your start-up professionally and confidently, at the same time encouraging you to understand your ideal customers and develop packages your qualifications and training your market expects. As a lone start-up it's all too easy to undervalue your offering, so investing in a successful business coach will save you time and money from the outset.

A Great Networking Group

Over 70% of business in 2015 was done via networking. With so many great networking groups to choose from, you can spend several months just getting a feel for the right group, people, location and format for you and your start-up. With networking comes support, business education, inspiration, motivation, confidence, personal development, useful contacts, sounding boards, colleagues, friends *and* great business opportunities. Need any other reasons to find the right network for you?

A Business Wardrobe

It doesn't matter which world you're coming from and into; it's important you look and feel the part. We all know impressions are made in less than 7 seconds. So, whether you're coming from a corporate background and entering an engineering, IT or cake maker industry we are all expected to dress smartly, professionally and cleanly! Confidence comes from within and a smart and clean appearance helps to magnify that. Your clothes and appearance need to reflect a business that is professional, reliable and concerned about the job they deliver.

Fun Stuff

Back in 1987, when Jim Carey had nothing, Carey used to visualise seeing himself having directors and people he respected admiring his work and wrote himself a cheque for 10,000, 000 for acting services rendered.

On Thanksgiving in 1995 he found out he was going to make $10m dollars for Dumb and Dumber.

Watch the clip here: www.youtube.com/watch?v=nPU5bjzLZX0

This time next year: What do you want to be earning? Go ahead! Write that cheque!

Print out the check, then fill in your name and the amount you wish to receive, in the currency of your choice.

*Jim Carey's Story
Look up Jim Carey's story on YouTube for he used a cheque like this to visualise his future.*

Success Stories

Here's what other business owners say about working with Clare and Meta4 Business Coaching. Start your success stories – who have you worked with in the past that can shout and share about your work?

Coaching has given me a new perspective on my business. I have achieved all I set out to achieve and more; I understand more about my ideal customers and have learned more about how to formulate a strategy that helps me do more of the work I love. In the time I worked with Clare I increased my revenues, won new business and developed a healthier work/life balance. Essentially, I now make more money but work fewer hours. I would recommend working with Clare to anyone who wants to develop an effective, profitable short, medium and long-term plan for their business.

Elaine Pritchard, Caittom Publishing

I arrived as a jigsaw puzzle, all broken into pieces. At the end of the 12-month coaching programme I gained so much confidence in dealing with so many small business day to day issues that are now not a problem. Clare helped me to put the pieces of the puzzle into place and so my business still has lots to work on but the picture is much clearer now. Clare helped my business to grow by 30% on average each month. Can't thank you enough!

Julie Hughes, The Village Rainbow

After attending one of Clare's workshops I decided she was the right business coach for me. I started working with Clare 6 months ago and the time has just flown by. With her knowledge and experience Clare quickly helped me to identify what I needed to do to take my business forward and she guided me in how to do this. With a structured approach I have achieved so much in terms of personal growth, business growth, structure, marketing, goal setting and forward planning. I now have a focus and a structure that will take my business to the next level. I would highly recommend Clare.

Sharon Taylor, Complete Harmony

I started working with Clare 5 when I really wasn't happy with where my business was. I always felt I had the potential, but something wasn't quite right. I was working myself into the ground and not enjoying working for myself anymore.

At the time it was a massive decision to invest in a coach. But I can honestly say it was one of the best decisions I have ever made. After working with Clare for 5 months I came away the happiest that I have ever been with more confidence and crystal-clear clarity on where I am going (which turned out to be offering a completely different service that I was originally). If you're not happy with where you are in your business, I would 100% recommend getting a coach and working with Clare. If you have any questions on how it worked for me I am more than happy to answer them. Thank you!

Tom, Fully Booked Marketing

I sought Clare's help when looking to set up my own freelance marketing business. Whilst at times my coaching sessions were a little uncomfortable – because Clare challenged and pushed me out of my comfort zone – she really inspired and made me feel that what I wanted was possible (which I had doubted previously). Having worked out my objectives we then went on to develop a detailed action plan with tangible actions. If I hadn't had Clare's help and support I really don't think I would have got my business off the ground with the self confidence that she has helped me to develop.

Fiona Pendleton

I appointed Clare to assist me with a career transition from being a head of a department in a national organisation to starting a business. I required assistance as I lacked the clarity of thought and purpose to understand the direction I wanted to go in and the specific tasks needed to achieve the transition. Clare was extremely quick to understand my drivers, my personality and my learning methods; and was able, from the first session, to create the appropriate coaching environment for me to immediately achieve my career change goals. I have never known such structured progress in such a restricted time period. She exceeded my expectations as a coach and I have no hesitation in recommending her as a coach." There are two lines from a poem by William Ernest Henley which sum up how I feel now: I am the captain of my fate, [&] I am the captain of my soul.'

Abigail Hall, Interior Designer

Having had experience of being coached on a personal level I was aware of the impact a similar process could have on my business. I also felt I needed an independent experienced sounding board to make sure I was heading in the right direction. Clare and I got on well from the start, and she was quick to remind me of my past achievements and how my wide and varied experience would assist me in my quest to build a business from nothing. Her own experience of starting out alone, having been in a large organisation mirrored my own and she clearly understood the panic, scariness and trepidation I was feeling at the time. Once we had set out our expectations and goals for the sessions, Clare challenged and questioned my own objectives and business goals. This was an excellent way of making me focus on what I was hoping to achieve; both intrinsically and extrinsically from the business. When two unexpected opportunities came along which changed my original plans, Clare was able to help me analyse whether the opportunities were what I wanted to do and right for the business. We are now focusing on long term goals to ensure that the day to day firefighting does not cloud the need for planning for the future, both for the business and for me. It has been a very thought-provoking process and extremely worthwhile. I would recommend Clare without hesitation.

Sue, Pink Mortar

Coaching with Clare from Meta4 Coaching has been an eye-opening experience both in business and professionally. Clare has helped me to gain clarity on the vision for my business, and think about what impact that vision will have on my personal life. Gaining clarity has meant everything to me giving me a renewed sense of passion, confidence and excitement about the future of business. I'm still a work in progress, but I look forward to working with Clare to take my business to the next level. Clare's passion to get results from her clients is evident from day one with working with her, she knows just what to say to squash those limiting beliefs and propel you forward to start achieving those goals that you have set out for your business.

Claudine, Tailored Communications

Clare is a superstar and I have no hesitation recommending her. I had always dreamed of running my own business, but for me the challenge was more about tying down all the ideas and mapping out potential options. Through Clare's significant experience and structured approach I am the proud owner of my own business and we're having a great time as we negotiate the start-up process. Don't miss the opportunity to work with Claire, she can help!

Adam, Impact Sales Coaching

Coaching with Clare has really helped transform my business to one that I am proud of and love being part of. Clare helped me understand & work on the things that were holding me back to allow the changes to begin…offering sound, constructive advice and tough love when I have definitely needed it! Our structured sessions have helped me achieve many things including re-branding my business, moving premises, having an open day party, changing my fees and introducing a membership scheme. My marketing plan is much improved and I am much clearer on how to get the best from things by setting a positive intention. I totally recommend Clare to anyone who needs to understand & overcome his or her business or personal challenges.

Lisa, Birmingham

Printed in Great Britain
by Amazon